CW00487210

1 MONTH OF
FREE
READING

at

www.ForgottenBooks.com

By purchasing this book you are eligible for one month membership to ForgottenBooks.com, giving you unlimited access to our entire collection of over 1,000,000 titles via our web site and mobile apps.

To claim your free month visit:

www.forgottenbooks.com/free153143

ISBN 978-0-484-58490-6
PIBN 10153143

This book is a reproduction of an important historical work. Forgotten Books uses
state-of-the-art technology to digitally reconstruct the work, preserving the original format
whilst repairing imperfections present in the aged copy. In rare cases, an imperfection in
the original, such as a blemish or missing page, may be replicated in our edition. We do,
however, repair the vast majority of imperfections successfully; any imperfections that
remain are intentionally left to preserve the state of such historical works.

[handwritten inscription:]

John Sidney Smith Esq
with kind regards
on the Author.

A PRACTICAL TREATISE

ON

AND MATRIMONIAL JURISDICTION.

DIV

I

A

PRACTICAL TREATISE

ON

DIVORCE AND MATRIMONIAL JURISDICTION-

UNDER

THE ACT OF 1857 AND NEW ORDERS;

INCLUDING

ENGLISH AND SCOTCH MARRIAGES.	DUTIES OF THE CLERGY.
SCOTCH LAW OF DIVORCE.	RE-MARRIAGE AFTER DIVORCE.
ENGLISH LAW OF DIVORCE.	JUDICIAL SEPARATIONS.
PROCEEDINGS FOR DIVORCE.	SUITS OF NULLITY.
BARS TO THE REMEDY.	RESTITUTION OF CONJUGAL RIGHTS.
EFFECTS OF DIVORCE.	WIFE'S EARNINGS.
PROVISION FOR THE WIFE.	RULES OF EVIDENCE.
CUSTODY OF THE CHILDREN.	AUTHORITIES AND ILLUSTRATIONS.

WITH NUMEROUS PRECEDENTS.

BY

JOHN FRASER MACQUEEN, Esq.,

OF LINCOLN'S INN, BARRISTER-AT-LAW,

HONORARY SECRETARY TO H.M. DIVORCE COMMISSION, &c.

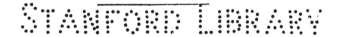

LONDON:

W. MAXWELL, H. SWEET, AND V. & R. STEVENS & G. S. NORTON,

LAW PUBLISHERS.

JAMES RIDGWAY, PICCADILLY.

1858.

Printed by EYRE and SPOTTISWOODE,
Her Majesty's Printers.

JUDGES OF HER MAJESTY'S COURT OF DIVORCE AND MATRIMONIAL CAUSES.

1. The Lord Chancellor.
2. The Lord Chief Justice of England.
3. The Lord Chief Justice of the Common Pleas.
4. The Lord Chief Baron.
5. The Senior Puisne Judge of the Queen's Bench.
6. The Senior Puisne Judge of the Common Pleas.
7. The Senior Puisne Baron.
8. The Judge of Her Majesty's Court of Probate.

THE FULL COURT.

A Quorum of Three Judges, the Judge of the Probate Court to be one.

THE ORDINARY COURT.

The Judge of the Probate Court alone, or with one or more of the other Judges.

When the Judge of the Probate Court is temporarily absent,

His place to be supplied by,—

The Master of the Rolls,
The Judge of the Admiralty Court,
Either of the Lords Justices,
Any Vice Chancellor,   or
Any Common Law Judge.

PREFACE.

THIS book opens with a statement of the English law of marriage, because the first question in every case will be, are the parties really united in holy wedlock? I say holy wedlock; for marriage, however entered into, is more than a merely civil contract. It is divine in its essence, though temporal and arbitrary in its multiform methods of external celebration. To use the language of M. Portalis, we cannot prescribe a term to it.

The law of Scotland as to this great contract, the parent of society, is also given shortly. Why? Because Scotch marriages may frequently give occasion for the exercise of jurisdiction in the new Tribunal.

It has been my endeavour throughout to vindicate the legislation as far as possible, consistently with right. I believe it will be found that I invariably urge a strict administration, feeling sensible that some at least of the remedies granted are but a choice of evils.

The duties cast on the Judges are more than ordinarily serious. For this reason the Act requires them to sift the evidence, and call for more, when they are dissatisfied or doubtful. This the House of Lords always did.

The great and difficult measure of last Session reflects credit on the Government, and also on the Opposition, in both Houses of Parliament; socially and morally, it is by much the most important and useful Act in the Statute Book. Yet is it very strangely put together. The labours of the pitchfork are visible in every page. Things having nothing to do with each other are placed in juxtaposition. Things intimately connected are far asunder. Not a few of the clauses are puzzling. Sometimes they disappoint by doing too little; next they startle by doing too much. Often we are at a loss to comprehend why what is plainly before the eye is overlooked entirely. Already grievances are felt which a line would have obviated.* Nevertheless, with all its defects, excesses, and omissions, this Act, wisely administered, has many wholesome and many admirable capabilities.

It is understood that the clauses giving a certain jurisdiction to the Judges of Assize cannot be worked. No orders are made respecting them. Local relief, therefore, is denied.

The question whether Her Majesty's subjects residing in the colonies or in India can have access to the new Court, is a question for the Court to decide.

Some things in the Act, too few it must be owned, are taken from the Code Napoléon.

In August 1856, Lord Brougham, ever under impulses of kindness, gave me (I being then Honorary Secretary of Her Majesty's Divorce Commission) introductions to the first lawyers in France. With these I repaired to Paris, and there, guided by the best lights, arranged the materials of twelve foreign codes with reference to divorce and judicial separation.

When my collections were submitted to Lord Campbell, as Head of the Divorce Commission, he at once determined that the Legislature should have them. He made a motion accordingly, and they were in February 1857 laid, by the Queen's command, upon the table of the Upper House. They were not, however, communicated to the Commons; nor did that Body hear of them till a stray copy came, by accident, into the hands of Lord John Manners on the 1st of August last,— too late to be of much service.

What is really excellent in these foreign systems may be said to have been almost wholly derived from the Code Napoléon, the preparation of which, in the Conseil d'Etat, furnished, says M. Thiers, a spectacle that attracted universal attention. "The First Consul, descending from his war horse, presided; attending every meeting, and displaying such method, clearness, and frequently such depth of views, as took the whole world by surprise. He had obtained from the Consul Cambacérès a few law treatises. He devoured them. In a short time, classifying in his head the general principles of Civil Law, and combining with the few notions thus rapidly acquired his own deep knowledge of mankind, he, by his thoroughly perspicacious mind, en-

---

* Thus all proceedings are at the outset to be supported by the complainant's affidavit. But this affidavit must be made *before the Court at Westminster*. No power is given to swear before a local functionary, so that the mere initiation of a case may require a long journey. *See infra*, p. 40.

abled himself to organize these important labours, and he threw into the discussion a large number of new and profound ideas." Napoleon at this period was thirty-three years of age; his chief advisers were almost all above seventy, and some nearly eighty. These men were selected for their learning and character, without reference to political opinion. One of them was Tronchet, who defended Louis XVI. Another was M. Portalis, a philosophic jurist of highly conservative leanings; and a third, the famous M. Boulay, whose practical understanding in some of the arguments vanquished and convinced the First Consul himself.

The constant topic of debate in the Conseil d'Etat was, how best to promote, and how best to secure the morality of the nation. The interesting discussions are given in the Blue Book; from which I have reprinted the Code Napoléon as to divorce and separation, forming Chapter XXVI. of the present volume.

I cannot properly close these remarks without returning my sincere thanks to many kind professional friends, and to some eminent clergymen, for the aid they have given me in preparing this work, which has cost more labour than its size may indicate. In particular I must express my deep obligation to Mr. Fleming, Q.C., Mr. Tudor, and Mr. Reilly, of the Chancery bar.

8 Old Square, Lincoln's Inn,
15th February, 1858.*

---

* Lord Lyndhurst has very kindly directed my attention to a note on divorce by Mr. Craik. (Romance of the Peerage, vol. 1, p. 408.) Mr. Craik disputes the now ordinarily received notion, that in the reigns of Edward VI. and Queen Elisabeth divorce for adultery was held to justify a second act of matrimony. With deference to Mr. Craik, we take it to be well settled that the dissolubility of marriage in cases of adultery was a principle adopted at the Reformation by all Protestant communities. The English laity acted upon this opinion. The Church of England sanctioned it. This is clearly made out by the Divorce Commissioners. Mr. Craik admits that "the side of the church which was in the ascendant in the reign of Edward VI. was in favour of divorce à vinculo in cases of adultery; and afterwards such continued to be the general feeling of the puritanical or low church party, but that party never was in the ascendant while Elizabeth occupied the

throne." Without troubling ourselves to solve the question of "ascendancy," we know this, that in the year 1597 a formal Canon passed in Convocation plainly discriminates between the process of *dissolving* and the process of *annulling* matrimony. The Divorce Commissioners, however, while they affirm that "the Church of England, as a body, disclaimed the doctrine of indissolubility," admit, nevertheless, that sundry individual ecclesiastics in the time of Queen Elizabeth held an opposite opinion, in particular the rigorous Whitgift, Archbishop of Canterbury. The late most singularly learned Sir John Stoddart, in his evidence before the Lords' Select Committee, Session 1844, lays it down, that "the Reformatio Legum would have been in all probability, if King Edward VI. had lived, the law of England. But although it was not the law of the land, it was the recognised opinion and sentiment of the English church at that time. It was drawn up by a sub-committee of eight persons out of the thirty-two, nominated according to the directions of the Act of Parliament, and at the head of those was Archbishop Cranmer; and therefore I apprehend that the Reformatio Legum having been published as a work of authority, although not of absolute legislative authority, it must have been, and in all probability was, followed; and for that reason in the Spiritual Courts there were dissolutions of marriage; because I believe that from about the year 1550 to the year 1602 marriage was not held by the church, and therefore was not held by the law, to be indissoluble." The abandonment of the doctrine of indissolubility must have been earlier than the date assigned by Sir John Stoddart, because in the year 1548 we have the famous case of Parr *v.* Marquis of Northampton, where it was held by a Commission of Delegates that the act of adultery dissolved the nuptial tie, and that a sentence of divorce by the Ecclesiastical Court following thereon enabled the injured husband to marry again, living his guilty wife. The Ecclesiastical Courts did not give sentences of express dissolution. They stuck steadily to the maxims of the dark ages as expounded by Sanchez. They did not obey the church. They adhered to their ancient form of judgment; they only divorced *à mensâ et thoro.* But in whatever shape their decrees were pronounced, the laity, in cases of adultery, relied upon them as justifying a second act of matrimony. Hence, no doubt, it was that the 107th Canon laid down the following rule:—That in all sentences pronounced for separation à mensâ et thoro a "restraint" should be inserted to prevent the parties during each other's life from contracting matrimony with a third person. What can this prohibition imply but that the marriage interdicted would have been valid if entered into? Bishop Cozens holds that the restraint was illegal. Mr. Craik, referring to Salkeld, censures that learned sergeant for saying "that a divorce for adultery was anciently à vinculo matrimonii." Of course we know, that in the Roman Catholic ages no human authority could rescind a marriage, unless perhaps the Pope, as God's vicegerent upon earth, had the power of dissolution,—a power which he but rarely, if ever, exercised. But with the Reformation, and apparently as an incident to it, the doctrine of dissolubility in cases of adultery was introduced. That doctrine was adopted in Scotland, not by Act of Parliament or by Canon, but by general consent of the nation. This seems to have been pretty much the case in England. Mr. Craik says that the case of Rye *v.* Foljambe did not directly relate to the law of marriage or of divorce. This is no discovery. The point, however, arose incidentally, and was decided by the Star Chamber. Mr. Craik says, the Star Chamber was not the proper jurisdiction; but surely Mr. Craik knows that the Star Chamber decided all kinds of questions. It was not nice, yet what it did bound all. This made Lord Coke affirm of this terrible tribunal, that "it kept all England quiet." Now, in the time of Archbishop Whitgift, Foljambe was brought before the Star Chamber for a riot. He defended himself on the ground that the land which he had entered upon was his wife's. The Star Chamber repelled his defence, affirming that she was not his wife, inasmuch as a former wife from whom he had been divorced by the Ecclesiastical Court was still alive. This decision reversed the law, or, at all events, the practical understanding of the law, which had existed in England from the Marquis of Northampton's case in 1548 till the case of Foljambe in 1602. In effect, the decree of the Star Chamber revived the iron doctrine of indissolubility,—a doctrine recognized in this country till the 28th August last, when the Divorce Bill received the crowning assent of Her Majesty.

I have been obliged to say thus much in consequence of the ingenuity and learned industry with which Mr. Craik has assailed a proposition which really ought not now to be questioned.

CHAPTER I.

ENGLISH LAW OF MARRIAGE.

CHAPTER II.

SCOTCH LAW OF MARRIAGE.

CHAPTER III.

SCOTCH LAW OF DIVORCE AND SEPARATION.

CHAPTER IV.

THE RECENT LEGISLATION.

CHAPTER V.

OF DIVORCE.

CHAPTER VIII.

EFFECTS OF DIVORCE AS TO RE-MARRIAGE.

CHAPTER IX.

EFFECTS OF DIVORCE AS TO PROPERTY.

CHAPTER X,

PROVISION FOR THE WIFE ON DIVORCE, AND INTERIM ORDERS FOR ALIMONY AND OTHER PAYMENTS TO HER.

CHAPTER XI.

OF JUDICIAL SEPARATION.

CHAPTER XII.

POWER ON DIVORCE OR JUDICIAL SEPARATION TO ORDER A SETTLEMENT OF THE DELINQUENT WIFE'S PROPERTY.

b

CHAPTER XIII.

HUSBAND'S CLAIM OF DAMAGES FROM THE SEDUCER OF HIS
WIFE; EITHER AS INCIDENT TO DIVORCE OR JUDICIAL
SEPARATION, OR AS AN INDEPENDENT PROCEEDING.

CHAPTER XIV.

SUITS OF NULLITY.

CHAPTER XV.

CUSTODY, MAINTENANCE, AND EDUCATION OF THE CHILDREN.

CHAPTER XVI.

RESTITUTION OF CONJUGAL RIGHTS.

CHAPTER XVII.

JACTITATION OF MARRIAGE.

CHAPTER XVIII.

MODE OF TAKING EVIDENCE.

CHAPTER XIX.

WITNESSES ABROAD, OR UNABLE TO ATTEND.

CHAPTER XX.

INTERVENTION OF JURIES.

CHAPTER XXI.

JUDGE OF ASSIZE AND HIS NOMINEE.

CHAPTER XXII.

ORDERS PROTECTING WIFE'S EARNINGS AND PROPERTY.

CHAPTER XXIII.

PROTESTS AGAINST THE DEFECTS OF THE DIVORCE BILL; SIGNED BY LORD LYNDHURST.

CHAPTER XXIV.

THAT FIVE YEARS DESERTION SHOULD BE A GROUND FOR DIVORCE;
BY LORD LYNDHURST.

CHAPTER XXV.

AUTHORITIES AND ILLUSTRATIONS.

CHAPTER XXVI.

FRENCH LAW OF DIVORCE AND SEPARATION AS SETTLED BY
NAPOLEON, FIRST CONSUL, AND HIS CONSEIL D'ÉTAT.

INDEX TO CASES CITED.

CHAPTER I.

ENGLISH LAW OF MARRIAGE.

1. UNDER the ancient law of England there were three distinct modes of entering into matrimony; the first, by public solemnization in facie ecclesiæ; the second, by clandestine celebration; and the third, by mere consent of parties.

2. Of the *first* class of marriages—those by public solemnization in facie ecclesiæ, the essentials were,—the publication of banns, or the obtaining of a license to dispense with banns; the performance of a religious ceremony in the parish church between the hours of eight and twelve in the forenoon; and, when the parties were under age, the consent of their guardians. These were the prominent stipulations of the Canons. They were simple and well understood, and they form the groundwork of our present ecclesiastical requirements, made familiar by the experience of centuries.

3. Marriages of the *second* class—those by clandestine celebration, now forgotten, demand a more detailed account. They were entered into without banns or license,—without consent of

B

guardians,—without regard to *time*—in the day or in the night,
—without regard to *place*—in a private house, or in a tavern ;
very often in a prison ; and not rarely, when it suited the impulses of parties, in a brothel.   Here we must explain a little.

4. Prior to the middle of the last century there was in the
Fleet Prison a colony of degraded ecclesiastics who derived
their livelihood from celebrating clandestine marriages for fees
smaller than those legally taken at the parish church.   Already
incarcerated for debt or for delinquencies, the reverend
functionaries were beyond the reach of episcopal correction.
In some instances their profits were very great.   Thus we
are told, that by one of them six thousand couples were
married in a single year ; whilst at the neighbouring parish
church of St. Andrew's, Holborn, the number of marriages
solemnized in the same period was but fifty-three.   These
clandestine connexions were also celebrated at Mayfair, at
Tyburn' and in other parts of London ; and, through the
instrumentality of hedge parsons, they were common all over
the kingdom,—in fact greatly more so than marriages in the
face of the church.   It is difficult to explain this, consistently
with even a moderate exercise of ecclesiastical discipline.   The
individuals who thus brought disgrace on their sacred calling
enjoyed, in some instances, pecuniary prosperity ; but more
generally, from their vices, fell into poverty and dependence,—
insomuch that a prosperous innkeeper would occasionally have a
parson on his establishment, at a salary, for the accommodation
of wedding parties.   The consequence was, that the bulk of
the common people, less awake to the terrors of spiritual
reprehension than mindful of economy, were joined in holy
matrimony by outcasts, who, though base and profligate,
were nevertheless, by virtue of their ordination, indelibly
sacerdotal.

5. By the agency of the "Fleet parson" the most unseemly
and deplorable alliances were daily and nightly effected.
Thus, if a man, in a moment of unguardedness or of intoxica-
tion, talked of marriage with an abandoned woman at a house
of ill fame, she straightway sent for an accommodating eccle-
siastic, who performed the ceremony on the spot, and was
ready to prove it afterwards when required.   An unwary
bachelor might be taken advantage of without knowing what
he was about, and yet be bound as effectually as if he had

gone to work with the utmost deliberation. Young men of rank and figure were frequently inveigled in this way. And the danger was not less but greater to the female sex, who stood more in need of protection, as indeed appears by many recorded instances. In the "Weekly Journal" of 26th September, 1719, we find that "Miss Anne Leigh, an heiress " of 200*l.* a year, and 6,000*l.* ready cash, hath been carried " away from her friends in Buckinghamshire by Captain " Pealy, a half-pay officer, and married at the Fleet against " her consent; the authors of the plot having used her so " barbarously that she now lieth speechless." Again, in the " Daily Post," of 4th May, 1728, it is stated that " two " Irishwomen were convicted at the Old Bailey for aiding one " Russell in forcibly marrying and bedding with a gentle- " woman—the ceremony having been performed by a Fleet " parson." The sacred profession of a clergyman was brought into contempt, and the ceremony performed made to appear ridiculous, by such occurrences as the following, which is set down apparently with approbation in the " Post Boy," a well-known periodical of the last century. The case is given in these words :—" A shoemaker having been carried before a " magistrate upon a charge of rape, and becoming sensible of " his danger, determined to compound the affair at once by " sending to the Fleet for a parson, who forthwith married " him to the young woman at a tavern in Smithfield, to the " great joy of all parties."*

6. The intervention of the Fleet parson made the clandestine marriage efficacious in the eye of the temporal courts by virtue of his orders—his priestly office—which no delinquency could forfeit or degradation extinguish. But what if a sham marriage were sought? The ceremony did not need to be performed within the canonical hours, or in a church; deception, therefore, was easy. A person in the guise of a clergyman went through the service. The seducer's object was served; the woman ruined. Shocking instances of this sort form the staple of old plays, and the stock in trade of sentimental romances. Perhaps the last instance is that of Goldsmith's Olivia, where the story is told with some inaccuracy in point of law. Circumstances so available in fiction must have happened pretty often in real life.

---

* 18 June 1730.

7. For the purpose of effecting these clandestine connexions nothing was required but the co-operation of a clergyman episcopally ordained. A minister of the Kirk of Scotland, or of the Presbyterian Church of Ireland, would not have been competent, for such minister is not episcopally ordained ; but a clergyman of the Romish Church was fully qualified to officiate ; as appears very clearly from the case of Beau Fielding, where a clandestine marriage, literally compiled of frauds and irregularities, was held good, solely by reason of the fact that the transaction had been sanctified by the presence and the aid of a priest.

8. From the State Trials we collect that the celebrated profligate Beau Fielding, who flourished in the reign of Queen Anne, entertained a project of repairing his battered fortunes by marrying a certain rich widow whom he had never seen, but of whose pecuniary resources he had prudently informed himself by procuring from Doctors' Commons a copy of her husband's will. To this lady the beau sent many tender and urgent messages, soliciting permission to throw himself at her feet, not doubting that if she were but once to behold his very handsome person she must necessarily conceive for him a passion similar to that which had seized other women on their first seeing him. The widow, however, we learn, took no notice of his importunities. But one of his emissaries, a woman of the town, having sustained some slight at his hands, revenged herself by persuading another of her frail sisterhood to personate the widow, and to come in that character to his apartments. This done, a Spanish priest attached to a foreign embassy was sent for, and performed the ceremony of marriage in the beau's bedroom, according to the rites of the Roman Catholic church. But it appears that within a few weeks after this clandestine marriage the beau contracted a second, a regular public marriage, with the Duchess of Cleveland, the well-known mistress of Charles II. She, however, soon found him an inconvenient companion, and determined to get rid of him by an indictment for bigamy ; of which capital offence (his other wife, the supposed rich widow, being still alive,) he was convicted, but pleaded his clergy, and would have been burned in the hand had not the Queen graciously pardoned him. Finally his marriage with the duchess was annulled by the Ecclesiastical Court ;—so that no precedent can show more

forcibly the regard that was formerly paid, in the temporal and in the spiritual tribunals, to marriages celebrated, under whatever circumstances, by priests, whether protestant or catholic, episcopally ordained.

9. The parties to clandestine marriages were sometimes not only high in rank, but eminent for virtue. Thus the great Lord Chancellor Ellesmere was married clandestinely. In like manner, the Chief Justice of England, Sir Edward Coke, secretly married the Lady Hatton, but for this transgression was dismissed with a mild rebuke on account of his "igno-" rance of the law." So says the record.

10. Marriages of the *third* class—those by mere consent, or consensual marriages, as they were called, had not the effects which attached upon marriages by clandestine celebration, and still less did they produce the consequences incident to marriages in facie ecclesiæ.

11. And herein lay the peculiarity of the old English law, when viewed in contradistinction to the ancient continental law. By the general law of Europe, prior to the Council of Trent, a consensual marriage was in all respects absolutely perfect. By the law of England a consensual marriage was good only for certain purposes. It did not give the man the right of a husband in respect of the wife's property; nor impose on her the disabilities of coverture; nor render her dowable; nor confer on the issue legitimacy; nor did it make the marriage of either of the parties (living the other) with a third person void, though it did make it voidable. Nevertheless, consensual marriages in England were indissoluble. The parties could not release each other, and either could compel solemnization in facie ecclesiæ. The contract, too, was so much a marriage,—so completely verum matrimonium,—that cohabitation before solemnization was regarded not as fornication, but simply as an ecclesiastical contempt. An act of infidelity was an act of adultery; and if either party entered into a second marriage, although in the most regular and open manner, it might be set aside even after cohabitation and after the birth of children, and the parties might be compelled to solemnize the first marriage in facie ecclesiæ.*

---

* Queen *v.* Millis, 10 Cla. & Finn, 534. See Lord Lyndhurst's opinion —his finest judicial oration, p. 831.

12. The interchange of consent might be instantaneous or immediate; that is, by words, whether written or verbal, importing a present contract, binding on both from the moment of the declaration; or it might be by words of promise de futuro, followed by cohabitation;—this last doctrine being recommended by its equity, and the just check which it imposed upon perfidy.

13. By the ecclesiastical courts consensual marriages were regarded as complete in substance, but not in ceremony, and the ceremony was enjoined to be performed as matter of discipline.

14. By the temporal courts, on the other hand, no marriage was ever considered good, either in substance or in ceremony, unless celebrated by some one invested with holy orders; that is to say, orders conferred by episcopal authority. Thus, if John married Mary by verbal contract, and afterwards married Elizabeth in facie ecclesiæ, the temporal courts held the second marriage good, and took no notice of the first. But suppose the first wife to go to the ecclesiastical court and there set aside the second marriage, and suppose the husband to be compelled to celebrate the first marriage in facie ecclesiæ; the temporal courts from that moment would adopt the first marriage, which they had previously rejected, and repudiate the second marriage, which they had previously recognized.*

15. Undoubtedly consensual marriages now and then inflicted deep injuries on families and innocent individuals, although the practice of enforcing them by compelling celebration under the terror of church censures, was intended and perhaps calculated to prevent treachery in the commerce of the sexes. Thus, by reason of latent anterior agreements, persons who had lived long and reputably together might be pronounced in concubinage, and their issue declared illegitimate. But the chief cause of the indignation entertained against consensual marriages was that they wounded human pride, a consequence not necessarily fatal to the interests of society. Some severe lessons were occasionally inflicted. Thus, a thoughtless youth of rank or fortune, entangled by a verbal contract with a " low woman," endeavoured to get rid of his engagement

* Queen v. Millis, 10 Cla. & Finn. 534. The question divided the greatest lawyers of the age. But the House of Lords ultimately *decided*.

by paying her a sum of money; and, fancying himself at
liberty, married a lady of his own station in facie ecclesiæ.
Nothing was heard of the first marriage until after the birth
of children by the second; when the woman whose claims
were supposed to have been stifled, suddenly started up, and,
by a proceeding in the ecclesiastical court, not only set aside
the second marriage, but compelled a celebration of the first,—
the effect being to bring ruin on the second wife and bastardy
on her children.

16. Towards the middle of the last century clandestine and
consensual marriages had together brought matters to such a
pass that the Government resolved to interpose. In 1753 a Bill
was prepared by Lord Chancellor Hardwicke, and notwithstanding a most violent opposition it passed into law, under
the auspices of a powerful administration.

In a social point of view this statute has proved more important than any Act either previously or subsequently to be
found in the statute book;* so much so that Mr. Justice
Blackstone, in a spirit of evident hostility to the measure,
pronounces it "an innovation upon our ancient laws and
constitution." †

17. To consensual marriages only a single section ‡ is devoted; and all that that section does is merely to enact that
such consensual marriages shall no longer form the basis of
proceedings to compel celebration. It does not say that such
consensual marriages shall be void,—which would have been

---

* Except the Divorce Act of 1857.

† It was extended to Ireland by 58 Geo. 3., c. 81. That the law respecting
the constitution of marriage prior to Lord Hardwicke's Act was identical
with the general continental law on the same subject before the Council of
Trent is the theory of Sir William Scott, propounded in Dalrymple v. Dalrymple, 2 Hagg. Con. 54; but that theory was displaced by The Queen v.
Millis. On looking again at Sir W. Scott's judgment we perceive here and
there symptoms of misgiving. The student will do well to read the Dalrymple case *first*, and then study The Queen v. Millis; remembering that
although the law lords were equally divided in opinion, the House, as a
house, decided the question not less authoritatively than if every peer
present had concurred in the vote. Accordingly Mr. Baron Parke, referring
to The Queen v. Millis, said, "By this decision we are bound." Cather-
wood v. Caslon, 13 Mee. & Wel. 261. See also Beamish v. Beamish, 1857,
6 Irish Chancery & Com. Law Rep. 142; but see 7 & 8 Vict. c. 81, and
12 & 13 Vict. c. 68.

‡ Section 13 of the 26 Geo. 2. c. 33.

the most effectual way of suppressing them. How far, therefore, they ought now to be regarded as valid, or as impediments to subsequent acts of matrimony, it does not seem easy
to determine. Anciently a person refusing to solemnize a
consensual marriage might be compelled by the formidable
writ de excommunicato capiendo. The clause taking away
that venerable stimulant was strongly resisted; but it was
carried with a high hand. And what has been the consequence? Ever since the passing of Lord Hardwicke's Act,
parties married by mere consent have been without the means
of compelling celebration, the modern law affording no other
relief but the opprobrious one of damages for breach of promise
recoverable by action.

18. The statute next addresses itself to the second kind of
marriages, —that is, clandestine marriages, — clerically but
covertly celebrated. It would seem that the suppression of
these was the chief object of this act, which in fact is entitled
" An Act for the better preventing of clandestine marriages."
And here, accordingly, the legislature goes to work in a
workmanlike manner, for it at once declares each and all of
such marriages null and void. And it enacts that the reverend
worthies who had gained their subsistence by celebrating
them, should, on conviction of further offences of the same
kind, be deemed guilty of felony and transported.* This of
course put an immediate stop to the Fleet parson's occupation.

19. But it was said that even the legislature itself could
hardly make void that which was valid by the law of God
and the law of nature. And it was urged that, although
every society might regulate ordinary civil transactions, the
solemn contract of marriage stood on a different ground; and
was not to be made dependent on a compliance with requirements for which there was no warrant in the dictates of
scripture, and no authority in the practice of the church
during its best periods; that a marriage valid in the sight of
God could not well be deemed void in the sight of man; and
that for an act of parliament to declare nugatory and worth-
less that which had, in all ages, been deemed binding and

* On the 16th Dec. 1755 we find that "The Rev. John Grierson was
" convicted of clandestinely marrying a couple at the Savoy chapel, and was
" sentenced to fourteen years' transportation."

religious, was something too dreadful to be thought of in a christian community. How these difficulties were digested by the reverend prelates is not recorded. But we learn that the government measure enjoyed their cordial support in the upper house of parliament.

20. It is curious to observe that while, as we have seen, the statute abstains from expressly nullifying consensual marriages, it declares all marriages celebrated irregularly, though before a clergyman, good for nothing. Yet such marriages were always of higher efficacy than marriages merely consensual.

The act having thus dealt with consensual marriages and with clandestine marriages, proceeds next to take cognizance of regular marriages, that is to say, marriages solemnized in facie ecclesiæ. Now here it is probable that the intention of the original framers. of the measure was to declare that no marriage should thenceforth be valid unless solemnized by a person in holy orders, and in some parish church or public chapel, according to the rubric. But we shall search the act in vain for words of this general import, although practically, no doubt, such has been the construction.

21. The statute rendered two things absolutely indispensable which were before only recommended; namely, in the absence of licence, the proclamation of banns; and in the case of minors, the consent of guardians. Borrowing a suggestion from the Tridentine decree, the statute further enacted that there should be two or more witnesses present at the ceremony, besides the officiating minister ; and an entry of the proceedings was to be made in a register appointed for the purpose, to be signed by the parties, the clergyman, and the witnesses.

22. It is the fashion to speak of Lord Hardwicke's Act as an advance in civilization ; and Scotland is charged with barbarism for having resisted every attempt to introduce it in that kingdom. Yet was this measure when it passed most unpopular in England. Not only the people at large, but some of the greatest and wisest of our public men, were strenuously opposed to it, and afterwards lamented its passing as a national calamity. Its practical working is said to have made good all that its opponents had predicted. The discontent is represented as having been nearly universal.

23. About a quarter of a century after Lord Hardwicke's

enactment, Mr. Fox, in June 1781, brought in a bill to repeal it. On that occasion,* delivering one of his greatest orations, he described the new marriage law as "tyrannical, unjustifiable, " oppressive, and ridiculous." He was followed by Sir George Yonge, who, painting in strong colours the mischief of all restrictions upon matrimony, denounced the measure of Lord Hardwicke after the experience had of it as a " very disgrace- " ful and pernicious law, not only impolitic but wicked."

24. Mr. Fox's bill was read a second time by a majority of 90 to 27. It was read a third time, passed, and carried in triumph to the House of Lords, where, however, it was rejected on the second reading ; since which time the people of England, more obedient than the Scotch, have come, under the tuition of the legislature, to look upon clandestine and consensual marriages as things not only illegal here, but of very questionable morality in those countries where they are still allowed. So that what Englishmen viewed with abhorrence 75 years ago,—what Mr. Fox and Sir George Yonge pronounced "tyrannical, unjustifiable, oppressive, ridiculous, dis- " graceful, pernicious, impolitic, and wicked,"—the Scotch are now held up as wilfully blind and obstinate for not adopting, at the recommendation of those very neighbours who so recently entertained and so furiously expressed such opposite opinions.

It is no doubt true that Mr. Burke disagreed with Mr. Fox and resisted his attempt to repeal the Hardwicke Act ; but the question is, not whether Mr. Fox was right or Mr. Burke was right but, whether it is reasonable in the English now to blame the Scotch for cherishing institutions which the English themselves adhered to so long, and surrendered so reluctantly.

25. The provisions of Lord Hardwicke's Act (in many instances productive of great hardship and injustice) continued to be law till the year 1823, when, by the 4th Geo. 4., c. 76., the penalty of nullity was confined to the case of persons *wilfully consenting* to the celebration of marriage before publication of banns, or before obtaining a license, or by one not in holy orders, or elsewhere than in a church or licensed chapel. The want of consent too, by guardians, in the case of minors, did not, under this Act of Geo. 4., invalidate the mar-

---

* Parl. Hist., vol. 22, p. 395.

riage; but the minister officiating was made liable to banishment. And the 23rd section provided that, in the event of any fraud practised to procure the contract, the party guilty thereof should forfeit all property accruing from the marriage.

26. The statute of Geo. 4. was certainly an improvement upon that of Geo. 2., but it was far from meeting with universal approbation; for, besides many other objections, it left the power of celebrating marriages as it had stood before, exclusively in the hands of the Church, a restriction which gave offence to almost every denomination of dissenters.

27. The consequence was, that in the year 1836 the marriage law of this country underwent a still farther mutation, having been then placed on its present footing by Lord John Russell's Act, 6 & 7 Will. 4., c. 85., which enables parties desirous of entering into wedlock to complete their contract without any appeal to spiritual authority. Such persons, therefore, as object to marry in facie ecclesiæ, may now repair to the registrar, and, upon giving the notices and procuring the certificates prescribed by the statute, may be married either before that officer by a verbal declaration, or, in the registered places appointed for the purpose, may solemnize their marriage according to any form or ceremony they please; taking care, however, whichever mode they resort to, that two witnesses be present, and that the proceeding be completed with open doors between eight and twelve in the forenoon, so as to afford some security for order and publicity.*

---

* See also the 7 Will. 4. c. 1., the 1 Vict. c. 22., and the 19 & 20 Vict. c. 119.

CHAPTER II.

SCOTCH LAW OF MARRIAGE.

1. The constitution of marriage in Scotland is governed by the principles of the ancient law of Europe, as that law existed prior to the decree of the Council of Trent; and it corresponds with the law of England, as the law of England stood prior to the passing of Lord Hardwicke's Act.

2. The Scotch *regular* mode of marrying in facie ecclesiæ, is by compliance with the orders of the kirk—orders easily satisfied, since all that is required is no more than a due proclamation of banns, and a clerical celebration in presence of, at least, two witnesses. There is no ritual, no formality. The minister admonishes the parties, interrogates them respectively, receives their assent, declares them married, utters a prayer, and pronounces his benediction. The proceeding is grave, solemn, and impressive, as befits the occasion. In general the ceremony, if such it can be called, takes place in a private house, never in church; it may be in the open air, and sometimes is. The attribute of regularity results from the banns. The celebration, a thing not enjoined by scripture, may be by any christian minister, whether of the establishment or not; and it may take place at any hour in the four and twenty best suiting the convenience, the wishes, or the caprice of the parties. The consent of guardians is not necessary.

3. The Scotch *clandestine* mode of marrying is by a clerical celebration covertly and irregularly conducted. The Canons of Perth, so early as 1209, describe a clandestine marriage as

one at which "a priest is present." The clandestinity is from the want of banns; and it must be evident that the officiating minister is akin to the. Fleet Parson already described.

But few examples of clandestine marriages are to be found in the Scotch law books. The last case was that of McGregor *v.* Jollie, which came before the House of Lords in 1828.[*]

A clandestine marriage, though under the frown and subject to the penalties of Scotch law, is nevertheless recognized by it as valid to all intents and purposes.

4. The Scotch *consensual* mode of marrying reminds us of the consensual English marriages, so tenderly handled by Lord Hardwicke, because founded in nature, and as old as our religion.

5. A notion prevails that marriages of this last description are common in Scotland, and it is even thought that no reproach attends them. Sir William Scott, when pronouncing his famous judgment in the Dalrymple case, observes that " the woman carries her virgin honours to the private nuptial " bed with as much purity of mind and with as little loss of " reputation as if the matter were graced with all the " sanctities of religion."

The same idea is evidently entertained by a distinguished living ornament of the ecclesiastical Bench, Dr. Lushington, who in his evidence before a parliamentary committee said, " he supposed it was but rarely that Scotch marriages took " place in the face of the Church, at least not very often, so " far as he knew."

Now there is not, and there cannot be, a greater delusion than that into which these profound and experienced authorities in this instance have fallen ; for in Scotland, so far are consensual marriages from happening frequently, that they are in fact never resorted to except where there is some disparity in the position of the parties, or some other cogent reason suggesting or requiring the temporary concealment of a connexion censured by the church and punished by the law.

Consensual marriages, as I have said, although viewed with disfavour by spiritual authority, and visited with penalties by civil jurisdiction, are nevertheless in Scotland, as they were in

---

[*] 3 Wil. & S. 85.

the ancient law of Europe before the Tridental decree, deemed binding and effectual according to the maxim, factum valet quod fieri non debet. It is material to observe that in this respect the Scotch consensual marriage differs from the consensual marriage known to the ancient English law. The English consensual marriage, as we have seen, was good only for certain purposes. The Scotch is good for all.

6. Scotch consensual marriages are either per verba de præsenti, or by promise de futuro cum copula.

7. The most remarkable example of the *first* method is furnished by the justly celebrated case of Dalrymple the wife against Dalrymple the husband. In April 1804, John Dalrymple, then a cornet of dragoons, afterwards Earl of Stair, went with his regiment to Edinburgh, and there became acquainted with Miss Gordon. The result of a short intercourse was a written declaration signed by both parties in these emphatic terms : " I hereby declare that Johanna Gor-
" don is my lawful wife; and I hereby acknowledge that John
" Dalrymple is my lawful husband." Another paper reiterated the declaration of marriage by the cornet, with a promise " that
" he would acknowledge her as his lawful wife the moment he
" had it in his power," to which she likewise in the same paper annexed a co-relative undertaking on her part, " that nothing
" but the greatest necessity, which her situation alone could
" justify, should ever force her to divulge this marriage."
Here then was evidence of a good Scotch marriage, irregular it is true, but valid and unimpeachable, though having no other foundation than the mere interchange of present consent,—without clerical intervention, without ceremony, without witnesses, without even the knowledge of any third party, and, above all, without copula,— the Scotch law declaring conformably to the old canon law, *Consensus, non concubitus, facit matrimonium.*
At the end of three months from his first arrival in Scotland, the young officer was sent abroad, and continued on the continent for three or four years; at the end of which period an abatement of his passion for Miss Gordon began to betray itself.

He returned to this country in 1808, and soon afterwards married Miss Laura Manners according to the rites and ceremonies of the Church of England. But now the neglected Miss Gordon determined to assert her rights, and took steps for the purpose in the Consistory Court of London, having jurisdiction over the defendant. The cause being thus entertained in an English Court, Sir Wm. Scott, the presiding judge, held that it must be decided according to the principles of English law. But then he observed, with characteristic refinement, that the only principle applicable to such a case by the law of England was, that the validity of Miss Gordon's marriage rights must be tried by reference to the law of the country where they had their origin.

Having furnished this principle the law of England withdrew from the scene, and left the legal question to the exclusive determination of the law of Scotland. The ground being thus cleared, he said, "The main inquiry was, whether by the " law of Scotland a present declaration constituted or evi" denced a marriage without a copula." In order to decide this point, he not only examined the decisions and the text writers of Scotland, but had the law of that country proved before him by the sworn opinions of divers Scottish lawyers; the result of which elaborate investigation was, that in 1811 he solemnly sustained the validity of the marriage. The necessary effect of this sentence was, that the English regular marriage proved a nullity, and the happiness of an innocent lady, nearly related to a noble family of the highest rank, was ruined beyond repair. 2 Hagg. Con. 54.

8. Another instance of marriage by declaration of present consent without copula, was that of McAdam v. Walker, decided first by the Scotch Court, and ultimately by the House of Lords in 1813. The facts were short :—An Ayrshire gentleman of great estate having taken into keeping a young village girl, had two children by her. On a certain day, in the presence of his servants, whom he had summoned into the room for the purpose of witnessing the transaction, he desired her to stand up and give him her hand, and she having done so, he said, "This is my lawful wife, and these are my lawful children." This done, he forthwith walked out into his grounds, and wandered about for some hours. On his return, the unfortunate gentleman committed suicide. From his previous character, as well as from the suicide, many supposed him to have been insane. The declaration of marriage, too, made by him so immediately before the act of self-destruction, and at a time when he apparently had that act in contemplation, seems scarcely reconcilable with the consortium vitæ essential

to matrimony. Nevertheless, there was evidence of present
and mutual consent ; and insanity, though alleged, was not
established ; so that the court in Scotland came, but with
much difficulty, to the conclusion that enough appeared to
constitute a marriage per verba de presenti. And this decision was affirmed under the advice of Lord Chancellor Eldon
and Lord Redesdale. Now, although the woman when she
stood up and gave Mr. McAdam her hand may be supposed
to have intended marriage, it is by no means so clear that the
man himself had the like purpose ; on the contrary, one would
say that his scheme was not so much to make her his wife
as to leave her his widow and legitimate his children.*

9. The husband may retain in his own power the evidence
by which the marriage is to be proved. He may withhold
that evidence entirely, or he may prevent its disclosure to
the world till after he has himself departed from the scene,
as in Hamilton v. Hamilton, where the man wrote a letter in
these words :—" My dearest Mary,—I hereby solemnly declare
" that you are my lawful wife, though for particular reasons
" I wish our marriage to be kept private for the present.—
" I am your affectionate husband, A. HAMILTON." This letter
was addressed by the writer on the back " Mrs. Hamilton."
It was not however delivered to her, nor does it clearly appear
that she even knew of it at the time ; but it was deposited
with a friend of Hamilton's with an injunction that he should
keep the document and shew it to no one ; and there was also
a significant instruction, that in the event of the depositary
dying, care should be taken that the document should afterwards come back into the hands of Hamilton only. The friend
on receiving the document from Hamilton, sealed it up in an
envelope, on which he inscribed these words : " To be delivered
into the hands of A. Hamilton, Esq., unopened." Some time
after Hamilton died. His friend the depositary attended the
funeral, and at the opening of his testamentary papers produced the above document, on the strength of which the
woman " Mary," to whom it was addressed, forthwith claimed
the character and asserted the rights of widow to the deceased.
The Court in Scotland held that her claim was just, and this
decision was affirmed upon appeal by the House of Peers.†

---

* 1 Dow. 148.   † 9 Cla. & F. 327.

Bowing to the dictates of Scotch law, we yet may express regret that courts of justice should be made to minister to the selfishness of a man who to the last moment of his existence retains the power of pronouncing his wife a strumpet, and who postpones the recognition of her virtue until his unworthy pride has escaped the humiliation of acknowledging her rights.*

10. If the declaration, though expressing a present consent, is not made bonâ fide, but is intended for a different purpose, the relation of husband and wife will not be constituted. The court must be satisfied that the consent is a consent really to intermarry, and not to do something else under pretence of matrimony. Thus in Stewart v. Menzies, which came before the Lords upon appeal from Scotland in the year 1841, it appeared that the defendant, a man of some figure in Perthshire, had made proposals to and was accepted by a young lady of ancient lineage in Argyllshire. For some unexplained reason he became desirous to break off his engagement, and to effect this purpose devised a scheme for the execution of which the law of Scotland gave facilities. In a word, he set up a pretended consensual marriage with one of his servants, a dairymaid, as an excuse for the non-performance of his promise. So far his plan succeeded. The young lady released him. But soon afterwards the dairymaid instituted a suit against him, to have the alleged consensual marriage with herself declared valid. This proceeding he resisted on the ground that what had taken place between them was not a marriage, but a sham, concerted to deceive a third party. The Scotch Court held that this was the case, and pronounced judgment against the dairymaid; and, what is more, the House of Lords confirmed this decision.

These examples sufficiently illustrate the effect of declarations de presenti, where everything turns on the reciprocal interchange of consent, entirely independent of concubitus.

11. Where again the declaratory words are not of present but of future import,—where they amount to no more than a promise of marriage,—in such a case if a copula ensue the

---

* See a further illustration, Hoggan v. Hoggan, decided by the House of Lords in August 1839.

relation of husband and wife will be constituted. This will appear from a single case. There are but few on the subject; the point having apparently given rise to but little litigation; for it is evidently a less strong thing to say, that a solemn engagement, relied upon and acted upon, shall constitute marriage, than that the mere ejaculation of so many words, without more, shall make one.

The leading case in the Scotch reports of a promise de futuro cum copula is that of Pennycook v. Grinton, decided about a century ago. The facts are thus stated by my Lord Drummuir, a learned Scotch judge, and a celebrated reporter besides: "Upon receiving," says his Lordship, "repeated " promises of marriage from John Grinton, Elizabeth Penny- " cook permitted him to have knowledge of her body oftener " than once, by consequence whereof she bare a son, which " he acknowledged to be *his*, and presented to the minister " of the parish to be baptized." It was held that these circumstances established an indisputable marriage.*

12. There may be a marriage in Scotland by what is called " habit and repute," and this on a principle eminently social; for if a man will introduce a woman to the world as his wife, it seems just that he should not be permitted afterwards to discard her, and declare her to have been all the time his mistress.

13. Thus, in Elder *v.* Elder, an exciseman had for twenty-six years cohabited with a woman in such a manner as to create a belief among the great majority of his friends that he was married to her. He invariably addressed her as his wife; went with her constantly to church; regularly slept with her; sat with her at the same table; and uniformly treated her in presence of others with all the decent proprieties of the married state. The exciseman, indeed, when sued by this woman for a judicial declaration of the marriage, attempted to overcome the inference arising from the circumstances of the case by the testimony of several witnesses, who stated their belief that he was a single man, because in official returns he had always described himself as such to the commissioners of excise. The court, however, held that there was "habit and repute" sufficient to constitute, or evidence, a marriage.

---

* Morr. 12,677.

14. The Scotch law, if it do not promote morality, has at least the effect of begetting circumspection; the hazard of unguardedness being very great, as appears by the last case I mean to quote, that of Forbes *v.* the Countess of Strathmore; where, upwards of a century ago, a lady of rank having indulged an intimacy with her footman, that individual sued her for marriage, and succeeded. The facts, as I collect them from a meagre report, were to the following effect:—That there being a prospect of issue between Lady Strathmore and the footman aforesaid (the plaintiff in the cause), her ladyship and he left Scotland together, and repaired to Holland, where she gave birth to a child. She afterwards returned to Scotland, and then dismissed the plaintiff from her service. This was an indignity not to be endured by one who conceived himself entitled to the rights of a husband. He therefore instituted against her an action of declarator of marriage; which action she at first resisted, but finally acquiesced in, the plaintiff's claim being apparently too strong to admit of successful opposition. No judgment, therefore, was required; but we learn from Douglas' Scotch Peerage, that on the 2d of April, 1745, " the Countess of Strathmore intermarried with William " Forbes," who, to save appearances, had in the meantime been advanced to a high sounding office,—that of master of the horse to the Chevalier St. George.

15. I conclude this exposition by a few words respecting what are called Gretna Green marriages; though these are not properly Scotch marriages, but seem to have originated from the passing of Lord Hardwicke's statute. Previously to that enactment, parties desirous of entering into wedlock might effect their purpose by sending for a Fleet parson. Hence there was no occasion for elopements; and such expeditions were unheard of, till, clandestine marriages having been rendered impracticable, the expedient of a flight to Scotland naturally suggested itself. It was known that under the law of that country a marriage by consent alone was good for all purposes. Therefore, if English parties could get the benefit of it, Lord Hardwicke's statute would, in so far, be defeated. Accordingly many persons, unwilling to risk the proclamation of banns or the refusal of a licence, straightway proceeded to Gretna Green, the nearest point of Scotland,

where, in consequence of the frequent resort of runaway couples, a sort of chapel was erected, and the matrimonial service of the Church of England was performed by the village blacksmith, who thus represents and now worthily fills the shoes of the superseded Fleet parson.

What gives effect to a Gretna Green marriage is the consent of the parties inhaling at the moment the genial air of Scotland. The mock ceremonial is but a ridiculous and profane superfluity.

We observed that in former times clandestine marriages were highly patronized.* And it is no less true that Gretna Green marriages have enjoyed good countenance; an Archbishop of Canterbury, a Lord High Chancellor, and a Privy Seal (all at one and the same time in the Councils of King George III.), having each of them, by an elopement, evinced his regard for nuptial restrictions; and by a marriage before the blacksmith testified his obedience to the law, and his reverence for the statutes.

It appears that the question as to the validity of Gretna Green marriages came first before the Court of King's Bench at a time when the greatest of all magistrates presided in that tribunal. Upon unanswerable reasoning, Lord Mansfield pronounced these connexions a fraud on the law of England, and they were held null and void. But, most unfortunately, the Ecclesiastical Court afterwards expressed a different opinion; and the Court of Common Pleas at a still later date followed the Ecclesiastical Court.†

16. In 1856 Lord Brougham brought in a most timely bill‡ to prevent these hasty and often disastrous border marriages. It provides that no irregular Scotch marriages shall be valid " unless one of the parties had lived in Scotland for 21 days " next preceding such marriage; or had his or her usual " residence in Scotland at the date thereof."

The statute directs registration, and contains other wholesome regulations.

---

* Supra, p. 5.
† Lord Brougham's Speeches, vol. 3. p. 462.
‡ Now the 19 & 20 Vict. c. 96.

CHAPTER III.

SCOTCH LAW OF DIVORCE AND SEPARATION.

1. PRIOR to the Reformation the redress of conjugal transgression by divorce à vinculo was not known in Scotland any more than in England. But after the Reformation divorce à vinculo propter adulterium was allowed in Scotland, conformably, say Lord Stair [*] and Mr. Erskine [†], with the precept of our Saviour; and none were more zealous in enforcing it than the Presbyterian clergy.

2. The change in the law was not introduced by legislative enactment, but by a sort of common consent of the Scottish nation. [‡]

It would appear that the laity in Scotland began early to avail themselves of a remedy so much favoured by their spiritual instructors. During the first forty years from the date of the Scottish Reformation (1560) many cases of divorce à vinculo for adultery came before the commissaries [§] of Edinburgh, whose sentences were from time to time reviewed, and

---

[*] 1. 4. 7. [†] 1. 6. 37.
[‡] Fraser on Personal and Domestic Relations, vol. 1. p. 654.
[§] The commissaries since the Reformation have not been ecclesiastics, but laymen; barristers of the Court of Session. Lothian's Con. Law, p. 14.

when necessary corrected, by the Court of Session, the supreme civil tribunal of the country.

3. In the year 1600 the parliament of Scotland passed an enactment declaring all marriages contracted by persons divorced for adultery from their spouses " with the person " with whom they are declared by the sentence to have " committed the adultery to be in all time coming null and " unlawful in themselves, and the succession to be gotten by " such unlawful conjunctions to be inhabile to succeed as " heirs to their parents."

4. After this Act the Scottish legislature did not interfere again, but the Courts went on deciding. The law of divorce, therefore, in Scotland is now matured by the experience of three centuries, embracing both principle and practice under a fertile variety of circumstances. The chief reported cases show the erudition of the Court in administering a remedy felt to be necessary yet perilous. Need we wonder that the adjudications are wise when we find among the judges the great names of Viscount Stair, Dundas of Arniston, Duncan Forbes, Kames, Sir Islay Campbell, Macqueen of Braxfield, Blair, Meadowbank, Corehouse, Hope, Boyle, Jeffrey, and Moncreiff?

5. Mr. Erskine (the Blackstone of Scotland), writing about the middle of the last century, treats of divorce with his usual good sense and erudition, showing the reasons on which the Scotch law rests, and the restrictions with which it has been found necessary to guard it.

" Divorce," says he, " is such a separation of married persons during their lives as looses them from the nuptial tie, and leaves them at freedom to intermarry with others. Marriage, being by the canonists numbered among the sacraments, is reckoned a bond so sacred that nothing can dissolve it. In the case of adultery itself they allow only a separation from bed and board, and even by our law neither adultery nor wilful desertion are grounds which must necessarily dissolve marriage; they are only handles which the injured party may take hold of to be free. Cohabitation, therefore, by the injured party, after being in the knowledge of the acts of adultery, implies a passing from the injury; and no divorce can proceed which is carried on by collusion betwixt the parties, lest, contrary to the first institution of marriage, they might disengage themselves by their own consent.

" As by divorce the nuptial tie itself is loosed, the guilty person, as well as the innocent, may contract second marriages ; but, in the case of divorce upon adultery, marriage is, by special statute, prohibited betwixt the two adulterers." *

6. In his larger work, " The Institute of Scotch Law " †, the same excellent writer observes :—" Divorce may also proceed on wilful desertion, i. e., where either of the spouses deliberately and without just cause deserts or separates from the other, and thereby defeats the chief purposes for which marriage was instituted. This ground of divorce is not only approved of by St. Paul, 1 Cor. vii. 15., but established by Statute 1573, c. 55., which enacts that where any of the spouses shall divert from the other without sufficient grounds, and shall remain in his or her malicious obstinacy for four years, the party injured may sue the offender for adherence before the judge ordinary ; and if the defender disregard the sentence, the pursuer may apply to the Court of Session for letters of horning to enforce it."

7. Divorce à mensâ et thoro is also known to the law of Scotland. Mr. Erskine ‡ tells us, that " if the husband should abandon his family, or turn his wife out of doors, or by barbarous treatment endanger her life, or even offer such indignities to her person as must render her condition quite uncomfortable, the judge will order a separation, and award alimony to her suitable to her husband's fortune until there be a reconciliation or a sentence of divorce." Upon this remedy the Lord Justice General of Scotland, in his evidence before the Lords' Committee in 1844, observes :—" I have never known it exercised by the husband. The causes which entitle the wife to it entitle the husband also. I have never known a case in my practice, so far as I recollect, in which the wrong alleged was adultery, and the conclusion was limited to separation à mensâ et thoro. The conclusion, I think, always went beyond that in such cases ; but I think that the conclusion might competently enough have been limited to separation à mensâ et thoro."

8. The Act of 11 Geo. 4. and 1 Will. 4. c. 69. enacts that divorce causes " shall not be appropriate to trial by jury." Power, however, is given to the Lord Ordinary, after taking

---

* Erskine's Principles, 85.   † p. 150.   ‡ Institute, p. 131.

the advice of the Court at large, to direct that "any such case, " or issues of fact connected therewith, be tried by jury."

It is remarkable that in the whole history of Scotch jurisprudence no instance is to be found of trial by jury in a matter of divorce or affecting the marriage contract. The remark holds likewise in France.

9. As already shown, divorces are granted both for adultery and for desertion, and the remedy is reciprocal, that is to say, open alike to husband and wife ; but we shall see that the wife seldom avails herself of it.

10. The total number of divorces decreed in Scotland during five years, from the 1st November 1836 to the 1st November 1841, was ninety-five, being nineteen for each year. Both parties in these cases were set at liberty to re-marry, subject to this qualification, that the union of paramours or accomplices is, as we have seen, by Scotch law forbidden.

11. Sixty-six of the ninety-five decrees were for adultery, being thirteen for each year.

12. Nineteen were for desertion, say four for each year.

13. Of the entire number of ninety-five suits, we find that fifty-five were by husbands against their wives, and most probably all of them, or nearly all, were for adultery, though the return does not say so. We deduce this conclusion because a wife deserts her husband but rarely, and in those instances she almost always adds a further delinquency which enables him more easily and quickly to get rid of her. It may therefore be inferred, with tolerable certainty, that in Scotland there are eleven decrees of divorce à vinculo each year procured by husbands against their wives for adultery.

14. On the other hand, forty decrees were upon suits by wives against their husbands. Of those forty it would appear that eleven were for adultery, say two for each year. Nineteen were for desertion, say four for each year.

15. Ten cases are unexplained ; Mr. Drysdale, the accurate officer to whom we have referred, observing, that " although " entered in the minute book they are not in the record." But he does not doubt their existence, and he gives a reason for their not being in the record, namely, that " they may " never have been extracted."

16. With respect to judicial separations, Mr. Drysdale says, "in the year 1855 I find two decrees of divorce à mensâ et

" thoro, and in the year 1856 only one, all at the instance of
" the wives."

17. This view of five years, being well authenticated, helps
us to reckon the business of the new Court, and more especially
to form some estimate of the probable number of marriages
that will be dissolved by it ; bearing in mind that the popula-
lation of Scotland is but little over *three* millions, while that
of England considerably exceeds *nineteen* millions.

18. It may be observed that the litigants in these ninety-
five cases were all, with one exception, apparently of humble
rank, chiefly small shopkeepers, petty tradesmen, operatives,
servants, labourers, and paupers* ; in short, the class for whom
Sir Samuel Romilly prepared a plan of divorce not long after
the French jurists, with the First Consul at their head, had
applied their minds to the same subject. See further as to
Sir Samuel Romilly's plan, infra, p. 129.

---

* The Commissioners report, p. 73, that "the average cost of rescinding
a marriage in Scotland is 30*l.* Where there is no opposition, 20*l.* will suffice.
In one case the entire expenditure was but 15*l.* 17*s.* 6*d.* From November
1836 to November 1841 (five years), the Supreme Civil Tribunal—the Court
of Session at Edinburgh—pronounced ninety-five sentences of divorce *à
vinculo matrimonii.* The parties litigant were almost all of the humbler
classes, including four servants, four labourers, three bakers, three tailors,
two soldiers, one sailor, a butcher, a shoemaker, a carpenter, a weaver, a
blacksmith, an exciseman, a rope-maker, a hairdresser, a quill-seller, a plas-
terer, a carver, a tobacconist, and a last-maker, as well as every variety of
small tradesmen and petty shopkeepers; but, except in a single instance,
(the case of a lady of rank against her husband,) not one of the Scottish
gentry figure in the list."

CHAPTER IV.

THE RECENT LEGISLATION.

1. THE Reformation did not extend to the English ecclesiastical law, which was allowed to stand untouched precisely as it had stood in the catholic ages. Marriage, consequently, was regarded as an indissoluble contract. Divorce à vinculo was prohibited; and the only redress known for conjugal transgression was divorce à mensâ et thoro, which was granted in cases of adultery and in cases of cruelty only.

2. In consequence of this state of things, a practice grew up, from a species of necessity, of appealing to the legislature for divorce à vinculo, where the parties aggrieved could afford the expense.

3. Under the administration of lord chancellors and law peers the remedy thus obtained, though in form legislative, had become, in truth, judicial, governed by rules, and regulated by precedent; so that the result might be prognosticated with as much certainty as if the question were one determinable by an action at law or a suit in equity. The lay and spiritual peers generally left all to the Lawyers. Proxies were never used. The Commons registered the decree. The regal assent followed as of course. Everything was satisfactory except the delay, the expense, and in many hard cases the terrible exposure.

4. Three distinct tribunals had to be resorted to,—a court of law for damages against the adulterer; a court ecclesiastical for divorce à mensâ et thoro; and the imperial parliament for a dissolving statute. This last gave the divorce à

vinculo. Each of these proceedings was costly, and all were humiliating.

5. Parliamentary divorce was a remedy for the rich, and not for the poor. To redress this crying injustice, the Queen, in December 1850, issued a commission to Lord Campbell, Dr. Lushington, Lord Beaumont, Lord Redesdale, Mr. Bouverie, Mr. Walpole, and Sir William Page Wood, to inquire into the law of divorce, "and more particularly into the mode of ob-" taining divorces à vinculo matrimonii in this country." The prominent question, therefore, was as to absolute divorces, and not as to judicial separations.

The Commissioners made a report,* which commenced with an historical deduction and concluded with certain recommendations, of which the following were the most important —1. That dissolution of marriage should no longer be granted by the legislature but by a court. 2. The the court should consist of an equity, a common law, and an ecclesiastical judge. 3. That dissolutions of marriage should be allowed to a husband for his wife's adultery, but not as a general rule to a wife for *his* adultery, although she might have dissolution of marriage "in cases of aggravated enormity, such as incest or bigamy." Finally, the Commissioners advised, that in suits for divorce à mensâ et thoro the existing grounds for adultery and cruelty should have added to them the further one of desertion.

6. In the session of 1853, the report having been submitted to the Queen, was by Her Majesty's command laid before the two Houses of Parliament.

7. Early in June 1854 the Lord Chancellor, on behalf of the Government, presented to the upper house a bill founded on the Commissioners' report, but materially differing from it. The bill was intituled "An Act to transfer the Jurisdiction in " Matrimonial Causes to the Court of Chancery, and to esta-" blish a Court of Divorce." It allowed dissolution of marriage to a husband for his wife's adultery, but not to her for *his* adultery. She was, however, to have a dissolution of her marriage when the husband, "since the celebration thereof, had been guilty of incest or bigamy." For all other conjugal

---

* Lord Redesdale dissenting, and giving separately his reasons.

offences the wife was to be content with divorce à mensâ et thoro.

After debates in the Lords, which are reported in Hansard, this bill, having been read a second time, and committed, was abandoned for the session.

8. In 1855 the public mind was turned to the Crimea, and parliament had but slight leisure and less appetite for legislative improvements. Towards the end of the session, however, Lord Lyndhurst stated in his place that the law of divorce would be considered by him during the recess, adding this important declaration, "that he saw no reason why the " system which operated so well in Scotland might not be " adopted in this country."

9. On the 11th March 1856 the Lord Chancellor presented a bill, intituled "An Act to transfer the Jurisdiction in " Matrimonial Causes, and to establish a Court of Divorce." This bill ignored the Court of Chancery. It allowed dissolution of marriage to a husband for his wife's adultery, but not to her for *his* adultery. It said nothing of bigamy, but it provided that where the husband, since the celebration of the marriage, had been guilty of *incestuous* adultery, she might demand divorce à vinculo. The clause allowing this had words of limitation, expressing that " the incestuous adultery " should mean adultery committed by a husband with a " woman with whom, if his wife were dead, he could not " contract marriage by reason of her being within the for " bidden degrees of consanguinity or affinity." For all other conjugal injuries the wife's only redress was to be divorce à mensâ et thoro.

10. Lord Lyndhurst moved, that the bill of 1856 be referred to a select committee, for whom his lordship, as chairman, with his own hand, drew up the following propositions. The manuscript was given by his lordship to the author. It may now be termed memorable, since it is, in fact, the germ of much that is good in the statute ; and the foundation of those well-intended efforts which have been foiled for a time by an over-cautious policy.

"Divorce à vinculo may be decreed in all cases of adultery, " whether committed by the husband or by the wife ; but " if limited generally to the husband's adultery, then it should

" be granted to the wife, at least in the following cases:—
" Adultery accompanied with cruelty ; incestuous adultery ;
" bigamy ; rape ; adultery with desertion for   years ;
" adultery and transportation; adultery and four years' penal
" servitude ; adultery,—the mistress obtruded into the common
" residence of husband and wife."

On the report of the select committee the bill was amended.
It passed the House of Lords, went to the Commons, and, after
having been there read a first time, like its predecessor of 1854,
was abandoned for the session.

11. On the 13th February 1857 the Lord Chancellor presented a bill, intituled " An Act to amend the Law relating to
"Divorce and Matrimonial Causes in England." This bill was
little different from that of 1856, as amended in committee.
It had, however, one feature of novelty, a clause authorizing
voluntary separations ; but its career was stopped by the sudden
dissolution of Parliament in April 1857.

12. In the new parliament, on the 28th of May 1857, the
Lord Chancellor presented another bill with the same title
and the like provisions as those of February preceding, but
omitting the clause as to voluntary separations.

13. This, the fourth Government divorce bill, though much
altered in its progress through parliament, has become law ;
a law, we must acknowledge, maturely considered, laboriously
discussed, and not hastily carried through.

14. It will be the business of the following chapters to state
and examine its provisions ; beginning with the clauses relating
to divorce. This seems the natural order, though not the order
adopted by the bill. And here we may observe, that the word
"divorce " is now to import in all cases a dissolution of marriage, and not a mere separation. Divorce, therefore, the
distinguishing characteristic of the measure, and the main, if
not the exclusive topic of parliamentary debate and popular
excitement, is entitled to the first, the largest, and the most
careful consideration.

CHAPTER V.

OF DIVORCE.

1. For the purpose of divorce, the Act requires that the Court shall consist of three or more of the following high functionaries, namely, the Lord Chancellor, the Lord Chief Justice of England, the Lord Chief Justice of the Common Pleas, the Lord Chief Baron, the three senior puisne Judges of the Common Law, and the Judge of the new Probate Court; this last, as Judge Ordinary, always to be one.

During the temporary absence of the Judge Ordinary the Lord Chancellor may authorize the Master of the Rolls, the Judge of the Admiralty Court, either of the Lords Justices, any Vice Chancellor, or any Common Law Judge to act in his place.—Sects. 8, 9, 10.

2. From this tribunal a husband may, on petition, obtain a divorce against his wife in every case of adultery on her part. —Sect. 27.

This agrees with the law of Scotland, with the Code Napoleon, and with the institutions generally of protestant countries. It agrees likewise with the practice of parliament, which has for more than a century and a half done for the husband by privilegium that which is hereafter to be done for him by a judicial proceeding.

3. The difficulties commence with the wife's remedies against the husband when he is the guilty party.

By the Scotch law the scales are held even between the sexes. In other words, the remedy of divorce is open alike to husband and to wife. The Code Napoleon discriminates, following the Roman law. The practice of parliament (subject to four exceptions, which will be noticed by and by,) has been to pass divorce bills *at the suit of the husband only.*

Under the Act, the husband's adultery, however gross, flagrant, and persevering, will not be to the wife a ground of divorce; for she cannot get a dissolution of her marriage unless she prove that her husband, besides being an adulterer, has also added one of the other aggravating offences specified in the bill. Thus,—

4. The Act allows divorce to a wife when her husband has, since the marriage, been guilty of incestuous adultery.

5. But there is a proviso that it " shall be taken to mean " adultery with a woman with whom, if his wife were dead, " he could not marry by reason of her being within the " prohibited degrees of consanguinity or affinity."—Sect. 27. This was not in the bill of 1854, but is taken from the bill of 1856, supra, p. 28.

6. The object of this proviso is obscure, and the meaning doubtful. It was not in the Commissioners' Report. It was not in the bill of 1854. Is it a definition? It defines nothing. Then does it restrict the remedy? If so, it excludes something. It excludes nothing, but includes everything that was included under the general word incest, used by the Commissioners' Report, and used by the bill of 1854, which bill was read a first and a second time and committed in the House of Lords without any objection so far as the word incest was concerned.

But it may perhaps be said : " This proviso has a purpose. " It is not a superfluity. The words ' *if his wife were dead* ' " limit divorce to cases where the incestuous adultery is with " the wife's relatives. They point at affinity only, not at " consanguinity. When the husband's incestuous adultery " is with the wife's sister it has been held that she is inter- " dicted from cohabitation with him, and that, in fact, such " cohabitation on her part would be incestuous. She must " abjure her husband. This is a case of greater hardship on

" the wife than when the husband's incestuous adultery is
" with his own blood relative ; because in this last case the
" wife's family is not tainted, and if she choose to overlook the
" depravity there is no legal bar to cohabitation. The inten-
" tion is, to leave cases where the husband commits incestuous
" adultery with his own blood relative to be dealt with by the
" law as it stood before the passing of the act, under which
" the wife might get divorce à mensâ et thoro. The proviso
" will prevent the new court from going further than Parlia-
" ment has gone ; for, although Parliament has given relief in
" cases of incestuous adultery with the wife's sister, it has not
" done so in cases of incestuous adultery with the husband's
" own blood relative."

This construction is difficult, and seems forbidden by the
words "*consanguinity* and affinity " which close the proviso.

If (which does not appear likely) the jurisdiction is to be
confined to the groove of parliamentary precedents, it is fit to
examine them. There are but two on the subject. Like
other precedents, they determine the case in hand, and nothing
more.

7. In Mrs. Addison's case (Macq. H. of L. 475, 594) Lord
Thurlow successfully pressed the wife's claim against her
husband, he having been guilty of incestuous adultery committed with her sister, so that Mrs. Addison could not have
continued cohabitation with her husband without herself
incurring the guilt of incest. This, at all events, was laid
down by Lord Thurlow, and was the ground on which the bill
passed. Lord Thurlow cited no authority for his remarkable
position, and it may be doubted whether any adequate one
can be found.

The canonists, indeed, put this question : —" Utrum is qui
" cum sorore conjugis fornicatur, cum uxore possit postea
" commorari et exigere debitum, ac solvere, requisitus ?" To
which the answer is : —" Nos respondemus quod uxor abstineat
" a commixtione viri propter honestatem publicam et in con-
" tinentia maneat, donec vir viam universæ carnis ingressus
" fuerit."

This is mere ecclesiastical tyranny, directed, moreover,
against the wrong party. The Council of Trent is cited, but
that council was never recognized in England. It would

indeed, require a strong law to prohibit forgiveness, and
interdict cohabitation between husband and wife. Sanchez, a
writer much relied upon in ecclesiastical courts, has sundry
texts on incest. His book "de matrimoniis," obscene and
imaginative, was meant for the confessional. It was, perhaps,
from this Spanish Jesuit that Lord Thurlow derived his
doctrine, content to use any argument to promote the cause
of justice and humanity.

8. In Mrs. Turton's Case (Macq. H. of L. 478, 687), where
the incest was, as in Mrs. Addison's case, by the husband
with the wife's sister, the result proved the same; but the
reasoning, as dictated by Lord Brougham to the author, was
less recondite and more satisfactory. The House of Lords,
advised by his lordship, then Chancellor, held that the relation
of sister-in-law, and of parties generally within the prohibited
degrees, was sacred. Hence the confidence and innocence
which marked the intercourse of near relatives, whether by
consanguinity or affinity. The husband, therefore, who violated that security, that sanctity, was guilty of an outrage
which entitled the wife to ask and obtain a dissolution of her
marriage. It does not appear that Mrs. Addison's case was
cited. It was not then reported, and it would rather appear
to have been overlooked, if not forgotten.

9. The Scotch Court has recently decided that marriage
with the deceased wife's sister is not incestuous. The decision,
however, so finding, has been brought by appeal to the House
of Lords. Should the result be an affirmance, the act of adultery with a wife's sister will not, in Scotland, be deemed
incestuous.

It is observable, that in South Australia a bill has recently
been read a second time rendering marriage with the deceased
wife's sister legal.

10. The act allows divorce to a wife when her husband has,
since the marriage, been guilty of "bigamy with adultery."—
Sec. 27.

11. The addition "with adultery" was made by the Commons. From the odd collocation, and the use of the word
"with," instead of "and," it may be thought that there must
be not only bigamy, but *subsequent* copula, or consummation
as it is erroneously called. This construction is not necessary,
nor does it seem rational. There must indeed be the two

D

elements of adultery and bigamy, but in what order they occur is immaterial. Suppose adultery committed by a husband with a single woman; then suppose bigamy with her; and suppose further, that as she is coming out of church after the ceremony she learns for the first time that her seducer is a married man; she renounces him immediately, and never sees him again. The case now put would, I apprehend, be a clear case for divorce under the Act.

12. What occurred in Mrs. Battersby's case (Macq., H. of L., 479, 667)? There the bigamy took place with a woman altogether distinct from the several women with whom adultery had been committed by the delinquent Battersby ten or eleven years before. The outrage was held, and justly held, to have been completed at the altar, although, to strengthen the case, subsequent intercourse was proved with the second wife. The trial, the conviction, the transportation, and the general infamy of the husband, were the things gone upon. Lord Cottenham moved the second reading, and the bill passed.

13. In Mrs. Hall's case, session 1850, where the like relief was given, there was bigamy, but no conviction, and, of course, no punishment, and less degradation; yet the bill passed.

14. At the end of section 27 there is the following rather dark proviso,— "and bigamy shall be taken to mean mar- " riage of any person being married to any other person " during the life of the former husband or wife, whether the " second marriage shall have taken place within the dominions " of Her Majesty or elsewhere." The second or bigamous marriage in Mrs. Hall's case was at Brussels.

15. The returns made to the Home Office show that the crime of bigamy has of late been increasing. In 1854, the number of persons committed or bailed for it in England was eighty-three; in 1855, eighty-six. It may now be expected to decline, because when divorce is attainable the temptation to commit bigamy will more rarely arise. Thus, in Scotland, where divorce is allowed, it appears from the returns that there were only two cases of bigamy for the year 1854. The population of England is six times as great as that of Scotland; multiplying, therefore, the two Scotch cases by six, we shall have twelve cases of bigamy, instead of eighty-six, annually in England. Here is something in the way of moral improvement.

16. The Act allows divorce to a wife when her husband has, since the marriage, been guilty of rape ; Sect. 27.

17. The returns show 128 cases of rape for 1854, and the same number for 1855.

18. The Act allows divorce to a wife when her husband has, since the marriage, been guilty of any of the unnatural offences in the Act mentioned, sect. 27. The number of these cases occurring annually is the subject of returns which may be cited by the curious.

19. The Act allows divorce to a wife when her husband has, since the marriage, been guilty of adultery, accompanied, or as the Act expresses it, "coupled" with *cruelty* ; Sect. 27.

20. In general, where cruelty appears, adultery is not wanting. The returns of the French minister of justice show, that in 1854 no less than fourteen hundred and ten cases of ill-treatment came before the courts of France.* Yet the most vigilant of all authorities informs us, that "there is more " brutal usage on the part of English than of French hus- " bands."—(Times, 6th March 1857.) It does not, however, follow that wives, even in the worst cases of adultery, " coupled with cruelty," will always demand divorce. A mother, especially when no longer young, will often be restrained by a consideration for her children from insisting that the marriage shall be dissolved. On the other hand, a sentence of mere separation is but an imperfect remedy, liable to be put an end to by reconciliation; such reconciliation being sometimes fraudulently effected by a wheedling delinquent spouse. Friends and relations will therefore interpose, and though the wife might herself be satisfied with a " separation de corps," they will occasionally urge a more effectual and permanent redress.

If these views are correct, a good many marriages will be dissolved by the new court at the suit of wives complaining of their husbands' adultery, "coupled with cruelty." The cruelty is to be such "as would entitle the wife to divorce " à mensâ et thoro."

21. In 1848 a case, that of Mrs. Dawson, came before the House of Lords, where the husband, an adulterer, flogged his

* Infra, p. 137.

D 2

wife, sometimes with a horse-whip and sometimes with a hair-brush. She asked a divorce; which, however, the Lords, from a regard to the morals of the country, deemed themselves obliged to refuse, in consequence, we believe, in a great degree, of a certain unguardedness, if not levity, which transpired in the conduct of the wife, unfavorably to her claim. Her case was before the House on six different occasions.

22. Some authorities on cruelty are collected infra, see p. 108.

23. The Act allows divorce to a wife when her husband has, since the marriage, been guilty of adultery, accompanied, or, as the Act expresses it, "coupled" with desertion. The desertion must be for *two* years. In many cases (those often of the greatest hardship) it will be impossible for a deserted wife to prove the fact of adultery. It would appear that the foreign jurists look at other circumstances, without always measuring the duration of the disappearance. And this shows their good sense; for a married man who elopes (say, with a female companion, to America) leaving his wife and children destitute, may be taken at once to have finally turned his back upon them; and, in such a case of adultery and desertion combined, we need not wait two years, or two months, to ascertain the culpable intent. The court ought to have some discretion in dealing with such cases.

24. In a bill prepared and printed for the Commissioners it was provided, that divorce should be granted to the wife where the husband had not only committed adultery, but had deserted her, *and refused, though judicially required, to renew cohabitation.* This judicial requisition seems a proper precaution; the Scotch experience shows this.

25. Some authorities on desertion are collected infra, see p. 110.

CHAPTER VI.

OF THE PROCEEDING FOR DIVORCE.

1. THE application for divorce must be by petition, " stating " as distinctly as the nature of the case permits the facts on " which the claim is founded ;" Sect. 27.

According to the practice of Parliament the petition should describe the parties, and state their respective ages, the date and place of the marriage, the issue, and the cohabitation.

Property brought on the marriage, and settlements made, and separations, if any, with the causes occasioning them, ought to be shortly stated.

In stating the charge, the petition will require a reasonable specification as to person, time, and place, and fuller than was usual in divorce bills, because the brevity of the parliamentary statement was compensated by the verbose pleadings and evidence in the Ecclesiastical Court, and generally by the record in the civil action.

Perhaps as good a model as any for the charge will be that furnished by the Duke of Norfolk's case (Macq., H. of L., p. 565), where the duchess having prayed that she might not be called upon to answer in the dark, the duke, pursuantly to order, brought in a charge prepared by his counsel Sir John Somers. The precedent is illustrious.

2. The statute does not require an answer to the charge, but if such answer be put in, there seems no reason why the court should not receive it. The Duchess of Norfolk's example is in point.

The case must be more than ordinarily simple in which the Court itself will not rather desire to have before it something in the shape of a record.

Parliament had always one and generally two records in such proceedings; so that the statements, whether written or printed, were never one-sided. The Scotch have their summons and defence, the French their procès-verbal.

3. The husband's petition may proceed on adultery alone; and the alleged adulterer must be made a co-respondent; Sect. 28.

4. For the intervention of the adulterer there is the sanction of the following precedent in the time of Lord Chancellor King: — On the 26th February 1729, Pendarves Kekewitch, Esq., presented a petition to the House of Lords stating that James Jenyns, Esq., had brought an action against him for criminal conversation with his wife, and praying that he might be heard by counsel on the second reading of the bill to dissolve the marriage of the said Mr. Jenyns, and that an order might be made for witnesses to attend to be examined on the petitioner's behalf, and that the second reading be put off for a few days. It was ordered accordingly. A few days afterwards, on the 3d March, it was "ordered that Pendarves Kekewitch (who " had liberty on his own application to be heard by counsel " against the bill, but did not appear) do attend this House " on Tuesday next." Of Mr. Kekewitch nothing further appears. He probably found that his attendance was unnecessary; for the bill, evidently a collusive one, was, without his interference, rejected.

The chief object of citing the adulterer is, that he may be mulcted for his delinquency in costs; see Sect. 34. An able periodical, the Solicitors' Journal, of 10th October 1857, speculates well on the consequences which may be expected to arise from the appearance of "a third party thus necessarily and publicly introduced."

The court may on special grounds excuse the husband for not making the adulterer a co-respondent; Sect. 28.

6. A wife's petition cannot proceed upon adultery alone. It must, however, aver adultery, and one of the other aggravating offences already specified, see supra pp. 30, 31, 32, 33, 34.

7. It is not incumbent on the wife to make the alleged concubine a co-respondent.

8. But the court, if it see fit, may direct that such alleged concubine shall be made a respondent ; Sect. 28.

This provision was introduced by the Commons to protect the character of perhaps an innocent third party from being blasted behind her back, as occasionally happened in crim. con. actions.

The appearance of the paramour and concubine as litigants in suits of divorce, although it may complicate the proceedings, and greatly increase the difficulty of decision, will procure for the new court a considerable share of popular attention.

9. A petition is not necessarily a written document. But supposing it ruled to be a written document, Sect. 41 says, " every person seeking a dissolution of marriage shall, together " with the petition, *or other application for the same,* file an " affidavit, verifying the same, and stating that there is not " any collusion or connivance between the deponent and the " other party to the marriage." But what if there is collusion with the paramour ? what if he has contracted to pay the expense, as in Mr. Downe's case (Macq., H. of L., 584) ?

10. Collusion, as laid down by Lord Chancellor Cranworth more than once, means a conspiracy or fraudulent concert to impose on the court and obtain judgment by putting forward a false case and keeping back or masking the true one. This was what the Duchess of Kingston and her husband did,—a juggle practised to deceive the court ; and not unlikely to occur where married parties, regardless of morals and tired of each other, are both sighing for liberty.

The function of the preliminary affidavit is to rebut this suspicion or imputation, by averring solemnly and upon oath that there is no unworthy compact ; that the suit is honestly brought ; that it is real, and not fictitious ; so that, whether well or ill founded on the merits, it is at all events fit that the court should entertain it. The affidavit, so to speak, is to open the portals of justice, but to have little and perhaps no weight in the ultimate decision.

Connivance or no connivance, on the other hand, is a question of merits ; not preliminary, but to be investigated in the suit.

Why, therefore, the affidavit should negative connivance, and yet be silent as to other misconduct, it is perhaps not easy to explain.

To connive means to wink at a thing. This is not a conspiracy or compact or joint act of two or more persons. Yet the affidavit is to state that "there is no connivance *between* the deponent and the defendant."

The oath in Scotland "purges the petitioner of collusion in initio litis." The same thing is recommended by the Divorce Commissioners; but they do not advise that *connivance* shall be purged. Lord St. Leonards, too, in his popular Manual,* seems to confine the affidavit to "collusion" alone. It is not likely that the affidavit, however worded, will be of much service. Mr. Ferguson, speaking of the Scotch experience, says the oath is "of little avail as a check on fraudulent devices." This is a reason for making it harmless, if not of use. All oaths should be simple and plain; and there ought to be as few of them as possible.

Every good purpose would be served by having the petitioner's signature, without any oath, attested by a solicitor on the spot, as is done in lunacy. But it has just been ruled by Sir Cresswell Cresswell, who regretted the necessity, that not only must there be an affidavit, but that it must be sworn coram judice at Westminster. The inconvenience will be enormous.

The affidavit will be not only often a mere thing of form but sometimes worse than a form, for it may supersede inquiry as to the real facts. See Goldney v. Goldney, infra, p. 115, and Greenhill v. Aitken, infra, p. 116. In Dr. Lushington's evidence (Divorce Commissioners' Report, p. 46.), he says, "it is all but impossible to prevent the court from being deceived."

In Scotland things are apparently worse. Hear Lord Cockburn :—"I remember a case in which I was moved on Friday for an early decision; and the reason given was, that the adulteress and the paramour were to have their banns published on the Sunday." Lord Cockburn indeed goes on to say, that he refused the application and refused the divorce. But the bare fact, that such an application could be made at all, shows laxity in the minds of the practitioners; and the truth seems to be, that the Scotch system, though good in principle and luminous in decision, is occasionally, when beyond

* Handy Book, p. 75.

the eye of the court, not a little loose in administration. See second series of Scotch Reports, vol. 7. p. 560.

12. The new court is not merely to judge of what shall be brought before it by the parties litigant. Sect. 29 declares that it "shall be the duty of the court to satisfy itself so far " as it reasonably can as to the facts alleged." The same section has for its marginal note the following words :— " Court to be satisfied of the absence of collusion." But in the section itself there is not a word about collusion. This defect, however, is rectified by the succeeding section; for there it is laid down that in case the court shall find that the petition is presented or prosecuted collusively it shall be dismissed.

13. One of the methods whereby collusion may be ascertained will be by examining the petitioner under sect. 43, which, in conformity with the practice of Parliament (Macq., H. of L., pp. 529, 537, 587, 606, 624, 633), requires the attendance of such petitioner when the court shall so order.

14. It would seem that a petition for divorce may pray alternatively for judicial separation ; and it may occasionally be expedient that it should do so, because the Court may hold the case sufficient for the temporary remedy, though not pro dirimendo matrimonii vinculo.

15. The parties, or either of them, may insist on having the contested matters of fact tried by a jury ; Sect. 28. We fancy it will not be often "that the parties, or either of them," will claim this privilege. But the Court, when it lists, may throw on a jury the labour of investigation and the perils of decision ; Sect. 36. When the judges differ in opinion on material facts, this course may well be taken.

16. When there are children of the marriage the Court will take cognizance of them. On this head see Chapter XV., infra, p. 79.

17. With respect to a provision for the wife on divorce, and interim orders, and other payments to her, see Chapter X., infra p. 55.

18. An appeal lies to the House of Lords against the decision of the "full Court," on any petition for divorce. But it must be presented within three months if Parliament be sitting, and if Parliament be not sitting, then within fourteen days next after its meeting ; Sect. 56.

CHAPTER VII.

BARS TO DIVORCE.

1. THE bars to divorce under the Act seem divisible into peremptory and discretionary.

2. The peremptory bars, that is to say, those which cannot be got over, are four; namely, 1, The having been accessory to the adultery; 2, Connivance; 3, Collusion; and 4, Condonation.

3. The first peremptory bar may be called *Lenocinium.* This word, though not in the Act, is a known and expressive term of art used in Scotland, and borrowed from the Roman law. It applies to those cases where the husband has prostituted his wife for gain or otherwise, and where he has been, in the language of the 29th, 30th, and 31st sections, "in any manner "accessory to the adultery." In such case the court "shall "dismiss" the petition for divorce; Sect. 30.

The phrase "accessory to" was represented in the House of Commons as belonging to the vocabulary of the Ecclesiastical Courts; but it savours more of the Old Bailey. It applies to the wife as well as the husband.

Some authorities as to Lenocinium are collected infra. See p. 112.

4. As to connivance, the second peremptory bar, a good deal has been said already in considering the affidavit which negatives it. Supra, p. 39. When connivance appears, the court "shall dismiss" the petition for divorce. Sect. 30.

Some authorities as to connivance are collected infra. See p. 113.

5. As to collusion, the third peremptory bar, we must refer to what has been said in considering the affidavit which

negatives it. Supra, p. 39. When collusion appears the court "shall dismiss" the petition for divorce; Sect. 30.

Some authorities as to collusion are collected infra. See p. 114.

6. Condonation (remissio injuriæ, as the Scotch call it), the fourth peremptory bar, means forgiveness and reconciliation. Divorce is privati juris. When the injury is deliberately and knowingly condoned by the party injured, there is an end of all claim to redress, unless the injury be repeated, in which case the original offence will revive.

When condonation is established the court "shall dismiss" the petition for divorce; Sect. 30.

Some authorities as to condonation are collected infra. See p. 116.

7. The discretionary bars are seven, namely, 1, Recrimination; 2, Cruelty; 3, Desertion; 4, Wilful Separation; 5, Wilful Neglect; 6, Misconduct; and 7, Unreasonable Delay.

8. Then, first, as to Recrimination. This plea is not admitted in Scotland. It was not admitted in the old law of France. It is not admitted in the Code Napoleon. 'If divorce is granted on the adultery of one party, is it to be refused because both are guilty? This is the reasoning of Scotland; but it assumes that adultery is cognizable as matter of police; whereas the injury is private and the relief private, and it ought only to be granted where the petitioner is himself blameless.

The Ecclesiastical Courts say that recrimination is founded on the principle of set-off. But set-off implies equality. Between the offence of adultery by the husband and the same offence by the wife there is no equality. "The difference," says Dr. Johnson, "is boundless." Accordingly the legislature does not go on set off, or compensation. Hence recrimination is merely one of the discretionary bars to divorce. It is not peremptory.

When the plea of recrimination or countercharge is established, the course to be pursued by the court is not defined; the only direction in the Act being that it "shall inquire into "any counter-charge which may be made against the peti-

" tioner ;" but nothing is said as to what shall be the effect of the inquiry ; Sect. 29.

The 31st section provides that " the court shall not be bound " to pronounce a decree of divorce if *it shall find* that the " petitioner has, during the marriage, been guilty of adultery." This discovery may not be on recrimination or countercharge. But it seems clear, that, as the court can withhold the divorce when it finds the fact of adultery on the part of the petitioner, it may do so more readily when the fact is not only found by the court itself, but made the subject of express defensive allegation by way of recrimination or countercharge.

Some authorities as to recrimination are collected infra. See p. 118.

9. Cruelty, the second discretionary bar. When established by way of defence, " the Court shall not be bound " to grant divorce ; Sect. 31.

Some authorities as to cruelty are collected infra. See p. 108.

10. Desertion, the third discretionary bar. When established by way of defence, " the court shall not be bound " to grant divorce ; Sect. 31.

Some authorities as to desertion are collected infra. See p. 110.

11. Wilful separation, the fourth discretionary bar. When established by way of defence, " the court shall not be bound " to grant divorce ; Sect. 31.

Some authorities as to wilful separation are collected infra. See p. 119.

12. Wilful neglect, the fifth discretionary bar. When established by way of defence, " the court shall not be bound " to grant divorce. The wilful neglect must be such as has conduced to the adultery ; Sect. 31.

Some authorities as to wilful neglect are collected infra. See p. 119.

13. Misconduct, the sixth discretionary bar. When established by way of defence, " the court shall not be bound " to

grant divorce. The misconduct must be such as has conduced to the adultery ; Sect. 31.

Some authorities as to misconduct are collected infra. See p. 120.

14. Unreasonable delay, the seventh discretionary bar. When established by way of defence, " the court shall not be bound " to grant divorce ; Sect. 31.

Some authorities as to unreasonable delay are collected infra. See p. 120.

These, eleven in all, appear to be the only bars to divorce under the Act. The writer hopes he has given them correctly. He has endeavoured to understand the legislation. He doubts his success. The court will decide.

CHAPTER VIII.

EFFECTS OF DIVORCE AS TO RE-MARRIAGE.

1. In Scotland there does not appear to be any express legislative permission authorizing divorced persons to marry again; but the prohibition contained in the act of 1600, supra, p. 22, against the inter-marriage of the accomplices seems plainly to justify the inference that their marriage with strangers is lawful.

2. The Code Napoleon, in stating the effects of divorce, does not specify as one of them liberty to remarry. It assumes the power to do so as a consequence necessarily following on the divorce; but it pronounces two important interdictions; first, that the divorced wife shall not marry till the expiration of ten months from the divorce; and, secondly, that the guilty spouse shall in no case marry the accomplice.

3. In England under the system of parliamentary divorce when the husband was complainant, he had liberty by an express clause in the bill to marry again as freely in all respects as if the divorced wife had actually died. Not so his delinquent wife. She had no permission given in terms. Nevertheless, as the marriage had been annihilated by the act, it was deemed a logical result that she should be as free as her husband. Some doubted this; but the courts were not likely to sanction a doubt which, if countenanced, might have proved fatal to the peace of many families.

4. When the wife was complainant, a clause in the act gave her express liberty to remarry precisely as if the divorced husband had died.   And in this case the delinquent husband likewise conceived himself entitled to remarry, and acted accordingly.

5. By the 20 & 21 Vict. c. 85. section 57, it is enacted, that when the divorce has become irreversible, "it shall be law- " ful for the *respective parties* to marry again as if the prior " marriage had been dissolved by death." This seems the only distinct effect of divorce declared by the act.

6. The statute, therefore, in effect displaces all previous enactments and assertions of nuptial indissolubility.   " It had " been deliberately decided by both Houses of Parliament, in " more than one division, after hearing all that could be said " from that (the Episcopal) bench, and after reading all that " had been written upon the subject, that by the law of " Christ marriage was not indissoluble ; and, therefore, the " law of the land was perfectly justified in continuing to " dissolve marriages as they had been dissolved for the last " hundred years." *

7. It also, by necessary implication, interdicts any proceedings against clergymen for solemnizing the marriages of divorced persons.

8. When a wife loses her husband by divorce she may enter into fresh nuptials immediately.

9. Now suppose a child is born within such time as to admit of its having been begotten by either the first or the second husband.   Shall the infant have a choice of parents, and shall the question remain in doubt till he determine it on attaining his majority ?   The curious case put by Blackstone, 1 Comm. 456, will not solve this mystery.   Says the great commentator, laying down the law as settled by decisions : — " If a man dies, and his " widow soon after marries again, and a child is born within " such a time as that by the course of nature it might " have been the child of either husband, in this case the " infant will be more than ordinarily legitimate ; for when he " arrives at discretion he may choose which of the fathers he " pleases.   To prevent this, among other inconveniences, the

---

* Per the Bishop of London, in the House of Lords, 24th August 1857.

" Civil Law ordained that no widow should marry infra
" annum luctûs ; and the same regulation was probably
" handed down to our early ancestors from the Romans ; for
" we find it well established in this island under the Saxon
" and Danish governments." If our ancestors, to prevent
these " inconveniences," as Blackstone calls them, required
twelve months,* and if the French require ten, how is it that
we are satisfied with three, or even a shorter period if an
appeal against the divorce can be sooner determined?

10. The proviso of section 57, that the clergy shall not be
compellable to solemnize the marriage of persons whose adultery has occasioned the divorce, is a compliance with a reasonable and respectable scruple, perfectly allowable in the high-
minded persons who entertain it.

11. The obligation imposed on them by section 58, as to
the use of their churches, is not likely to be often the subject
of requisition, inasmuch as divorced persons, seeking fresh
nuptials, will go beyond the smoke of their own dwellings.

12. This topic was excellently handled by the Bishop of
London, on the 24th of August last, when, as a spiritual
peer of Parliament, he expressed himself in the following
terms : — " Although he (the right reverend prelate), and
" a vast number of the clergy, maintained that marriage
" was not indissoluble by the law of Christ ; that adultery
" was so heinous a crime that in itself it dissolved marriage ;
" it was quite consistent for them to wish that they should
" not be obliged to use all the expressions of the marriage
" service in the re-marriage of persons divorced for adul-
" tery. Their lordships had already on four divisions shown
" their indisposition to allow an exemption to the clergy from
" the obligation of marrying divorced persons ; and the bill
" went down to the Lower House without any such exemption.
" Surely the clergy, if they were anxious for this exemption,
" ought to be very thankful that they had got it from the
" House of Commons, for it was generally believed that the
" feelings of the clergy were more respected by their lordships
" than by the other branch of the legislature. For his own
" part, if he were asked his opinion, he would advise the
" clergy to accept the compromise which the bill offered to

---

* Sit omnis vidua sine marito duodecim menses. — LL. Ethelr. A.D. 1008 ;
LL. Canut. c. 71.

" them.   If the bill were to be thrown over for three or six
" months, and another session were to be (he would not say
" wasted, but) mis-spent, in discussions of a kind by no means
" calculated to promote public morality, he was afraid their
" claims would not be so readily acknowledged as they had been.
" To allow a clergyman to go into another man's parish to cele--
" brate marriage was undoubtedly something new ; but so
" was the exemption, for the clergy had hitherto been obliged
" to re-marry divorced persons.   Moreover, he did not think
" it was very likely that parties would be so glad to make a
" parade of their sin, or their misfortune, as to go to their
" own clergyman and request to be married in his parish
" church ; and it was extremely unlikely that, in the event of
" his refusing to officiate himself, they would seek to bring
" in his next neighbour.   He (the right reverend prelate)
" believed that the provision in the bill with respect to
" parish churches had been introduced, not with any idea
" that it would ever be practically useful, but because of cer-
" tain strong language employed in both houses, which had
" created an impression that the clergy wanted to dominate.
" Hence he believed it was that the House of Commons
" insisted on having a recognition of the principle that the
" parish churches belonged to the laity as well as to the
" clergy ; and, when the representatives of the people were
" making a great, and he thought a just, concession to a
" proper feeling on the part of the clergy, they desired, on the
" other hand, to be able to point to something which would
" show their assertion of independence.   His advice, therefore,
" to the clergy was, that they should receive the exemption
" with the condition which had been annexed to it."

13. After this admirable advice, which is also a caution,
it is with no slight satisfaction that we find another right
reverend prelate, the very learned and acute Bishop of Exeter,
candidly avowing that he does not anticipitate any *practical*
evil whatever from the enactment, although, no doubt, in
principle, he considers it open to very great complaint ; his
lordship, however, gives us an important consolation, derived
from his truly legal examination of the 58th section, namely,
that if mischief had really been intended, " the wording of the
" clause would have been different, for in that case any clergy-
" man whatever would have been permitted to perform the

E

" marriage service, instead of any minister entitled to officiate
" within the diocese." This his lordship holds to be " no slight
security," and he trusts that no incumbent or curate of his
diocese "will incur the odium which would most justly attach
" to a clergyman intruding into the church of another for the
" purpose of performing a service which the proper minister
" deems unfit to be performed in it."*

14. A third most eloquent bishop, in a sterner mood, issues
a mandate to the surrogates of his diocese, that they do not
grant a licence for marriage to any divorced person, " if the
husband or wife of such divorced person be still alive."

15. Is the surrogate bound or entitled to inquire whether
" the husband or wife of the divorced person be still alive?"
Can he put the parties to the proof? He may give a little
trouble.   But where is the gain to the clergy?   Parochial
duty must be performed in spite of surrogates. Banns must
be published if the parties insist. But the contingency will
never arise, for they can very easily go to another district;
and there, according to some opinions, make reparation for
their sin, or cure their misfortune.

16. In large towns a clergyman has no knowledge whether
John Jackson or Lavinia Tompkins, who appears before him
for matrimony, has or has not been previously married, and
previously divorced. The man will present himself as a
bachelor; the woman will come, not as a married person,
or as a widow, but as a spinster. In a word, the sentence
of divorce will effectually restore the parties to their original
single state.

17. And here a question arises. Shall the wife invariably
after divorce resume her maiden or other former name?
Supposing there are no children, it would seem that she
may do so expediently. But if there are children, and if
they, or some of them, are committed to her care, the decision of a thoughtful mother would probably be different.
The Act is silent.

* Letter to the Archdeacon of Barnstaple, Nov. 23, 1857; published in
the Guardian.

CHAPTER IX.

EFFECTS OF DIVORCE AS TO PROPERTY.

1. THE Scotch law has the following rules : Says the Lord Viscount Stair :—" 1. On divorce, the party injurer loses all " benefit accruing through the marriage. 2. The party in-" jured has the same benefit as by the other's natural death." And Mr. Bell adds, " 1. The guilty party is barred from " claiming any benefit from the *dissolution* of the marriage. " 2. The innocent party can claim no interest in any estate " afterwards acquired by the guilty party. 3. The rights of " parties are fixed as at the date of the decree. 4. Death " before the decree prevents these consequences."

2. The provisions of the Code Napoleon are infra, Arts. 47 and 48, p. 134.

3. In all private divorce bills it was the practice to intro-duce certain clauses regulating consequences. This practice commenced with the Duke of Norfolk's case in 1692, and continued without one exception to the present time.

4. Thus, when the husband was complainant, the enacting clauses were the following :—

5. In the first place, there was a clause providing that, should he marry again, he should be entitled to all the rights of a husband as regarded the property of his after-taken wife, and that she, on the other hand, should, with respect to *his* property, be entitled to all the rights of a wife precisely as if her predecessor, instead of being divorced, had departed this life.

6. Then there was a clause whereby the divorced wife was barred of dower* and freebench, and the distributive share of her husband's personalty, which, but for the act, would have accrued to her as widow in the event of her survivorship.

7. The last property clause in a divorce bill, where the husband was complainant, excluded him from all claim on any property which might come to his divorced wife "after" the dissolution of the marriage.

8. While, by these clauses, the divorced wife was barred of all claim upon her injured husband's property, whether enjoyed by him before the divorce, or coming to him after it, the exclusion of his claim upon *her* property was limited to property acquired by her after the passing of the bill. Thus much when the husband was complainant.

9. When, again, the wife was complainant, there was a clause enacting, that if she married again, she and her after-taken husband should have the same rights as if the divorced husband had died.

10. Another clause provided that the divorced husband should be barred of all claim on the injured wife's estates, goods, chattels, and personal ornaments "enjoyed by her in "possession in her own right," or which she might afterwards in any way acquire.

11. So far as her own property was concerned she was restored to the position in which she had stood prior to her ·marriage.

But there was no provision made to determine what her rights should be with respect to the property of her divorced husband. For anything appearing to the contrary, she might

---

* One would think the Statute of Westminster the Second had effectually done this already.

still, notwithstanding the divorce, claim dower and freebench at his death, and her distributive share of his personalty.

12. The cases which were thus usually provided for by private bills of divorce do not appear to have been provided for by the recent act of general legislation.

13. It would seem, therefore, that questions may now arise which were formerly anticipated and obviated.

There may also spring up another set of questions, some of which occurred and were found not to have been guarded against by the provisions of private divorce bills. The following are samples :—

14. If, by settlement, the wife were entitled to pin-money limited during the joint lives, would such pin-money stop on divorce ?

15. If, by settlement, the wife were entitled to a jointure on surviving her husband, would such jointure be demandable on divorce ? Would it be demandable on the husband's death ? The divorced wife would not then fill the character in which it was meant that she should enjoy it. Suppose the husband to be tenant for life with a power of jointuring, and that he has jointured ; then suppose that he divorces his wife, marries again, jointures again, and dies, leaving his two wives him surviving ; which is to claim ? or can either ?

16. Upon the sentence of divorce what shall become of the divorced wife's ante-nuptial debts ? The husband, although legally answerable for them during the coverture, cannot be charged with them after her death. Now, shall the same consequence take place when the marriage is dissolved, not by the wife's death, but by divorce ? Shall the husband be allowed to keep her property, and yet be absolved from her engagements ?

17. Under the common law, on the dissolution of the marriage by the husband's death, the liability of the wife to personal demand and personal execution, in respect of debts contracted by her when sole, revives. Is the same consequence to ensue on divorce ?

18. The practice of parliament on private bills of divorce was, to declare that the husband should have no claim on the divorced wife's *after-acquired* property, leaving him to retain all such property of his wife's as passed to him absolutely *jure mariti*. But how will the law now stand respecting such

parts of the wife's property as came under his dominion, but did not by the marriage become the absolute property of the husband ? Will he, notwithstanding the divorce, be entitled to receive the rents and profits of her real estate during their joint lives ? And will he be tenant by the curtesy after her death, supposing that he would have been such had there been no divorce ? Of her chattels will he have the enjoyment and disposition? Shall his right to reduce her choses in action into possession continue notwithstanding the divorce ? or shall they belong to the wife, as they would in the case of her survivorship ?

19. When the wife's estates were, during the coverture, mortgaged for the husband's debts, shall he, on the divorce, supposing him to have been the injured party, be entitled to resist her demand of redemption and exoneration ?

20· When the wife has property to her separate use, shall the injured husband have any claim upon it at her death, supposing her to leave it undisposed of by will or otherwise ?

21. If divorces become numerous, questions on the consequences will multiply. It may be said the court can impose terms on the party seeking the remedy, as we shall see by the next chapter, but no bargain can be imposed on the respondent. The court cannot legislate, nor can any human registrar prepare decrees adequate to meet the circumstances of every case.

22. On the whole it seems not easy to say what shall be the effects of divorce as to property under 20 & 21 Vict. c. 85.

23. Some authorities are collected infra. See p. 121.

CHAPTER X.

PROVISION FOR THE WIFE ON DIVORCE, AND INTERIM ORDERS FOR ALIMONY AND OTHER PAYMENTS TO HER.

1. THE parliamentary practice of requiring the injured husband to make a provision for his delinquent wife had not much to recommend it, either morally or legally. Morally, it seems monstrous to compel a man to support through life the woman who has dishonoured him; legally, she has no claim whatever, because after she has committed adultery, her husband may turn her out of doors. By the law of France she is viewed as a criminal and punished; and many whose opinions are entitled to great respect think the French law right. What therefore can appear more strange than to call upon the husband to secure her a maintenance? Yet this was constantly done in parliament, sometimes in the upper but oftener in the lower assembly.

2. The usage commenced at an early period, when the complainants were generally men of figure and station, whose wives, though culpable, had in the legislative body relatives and friends who stood out for terms,—divorce being a bounty unknown to the law.

3. Moreover some early divorce bills were passed, through influence, at the suit of husbands who were content to submit to any conditions that the advisers of the lady might propose. In this way the thing originated; and in this way, what was

no doubt startling at first, came in time to be regarded as not wholly unreasonable, especially where the wife was of high rank, where she had brought a fortune to the husband, and where withal her defection was accompanied by palliating circumstances.

4. But parliament made it ultimately a positive rule, in all cases, to impose this humiliating burden; and the Commons had, and perhaps still have, a functionary appointed to watch the delinquent wife's interest and make stipulations for her. The performance of this duty was an object of ambition in the house. The senator chosen for the post was designated "The Lady's Friend."

5. The following is the form of the bond ordinarily insisted upon by the "Lady's Friend :"—

KNOW all men by these presents, that I,   , am held and firmly bound to   , his executors, administrators, and assigns, in the sum of   , to be paid to the said   , his executors, administrators, or assigns, for which payment to be well and truly made I bind myself, my heirs, executors, and administrators, firmly by these presents, sealed with my seal, and dated this fourteenth day of July, one thousand eight hundred and fifty-seven, and in the twenty-first year of the reign of Queen Victoria.

Whereas a bill is now pending in parliament to dissolve the marriage of the above bounden   with his present wife   , and for other purposes. Now the condition of the above-written bond or obligation is such, that if the said   do and shall well and truly pay or cause to be paid to the said   during the life of the said   his now wife, one annuity or yearly sum of   , by equal half-yearly payments, on the   day of   and the   day of   in every year, with a proportionate part thereof up to the day of the decease of the said   , the first half-yearly payment thereof to be made on the   day of   next ensuing the date of the above-written bond; or if the said recited bill shall not come into law, then above-written bond or obligation to be void, otherwise to be and remain in full force and virtue.

Signed, sealed, and delivered,
&c.

Thus every half year the unfortunate husband was to be reminded of his calamity.

6. In Mr. Loveden's case (Macq., H. of L., p. 606), the Commons made an amendment on the bill, compelling him to allow Mrs. Loveden 400l. a year for life, although she was at the time living openly with her paramour. Mr. Loveden, by

petition, represented that the amendment had "a manifest tendency to loosen the bonds of conjugal fidelity, and that the allowing it would be a premium to wives for the commission of adultery." This shared the usual fate of unanswerable arguments—it made no impression ; and, as Mr. Loveden refused compliance, his bill was rejected.

7. But whatever might have been said or thought under the system of parliamentary divorce, the question assumes an entirely different aspect now that the remedy has become a legal one demandable ex debito justitiæ.

8. With respect to the practice of Scotland, the very learned Professor More writes to me :—"There is not an " instance, so far as I am aware, of our courts having ever " required a husband to make a provision for his adulterous " wife, or of making that a condition of granting the divorce. " On the contrary, it has been held, that if the wife were an " *heiress*, the husband might, by virtue of his courtesy, claim " the rents of her lands, as if she were naturally dead ; and " it has also been decided that the wife cannot claim even " the return of her tocher (fortune)."— See *Morison's Dictionary* voce *Adultery*, pp. 329 and 333.

9. By the late act, section thirty-two, the court on divorce " may order that the husband shall secure to the wife such " gross sum of money, or such annual sum of money for any " term not exceeding her own life, as it shall deem reasonable ; " and it may suspend its decree until a deed for the purpose " shall have been duly executed." The suspension of the decree would prove a stimulus only where the husband was the complainant and the wife the delinquent. Therefore the act contemplates a continuance of the parliamentary practice at the discretion of the court.

10. Under this section the guilty wife may be advised to petition the court for a provision, following therein the examples of the Duchess of Norfolk (Macq., H. of L., 572), and of Lady Elizabeth Howard (Lords' Journals, 21st March 1794).

11. In Mr. Tyrrell's case (Macq., H. of L., 644), the counsel for Mrs. Tyrrell represented that, after having brought 45,000*l.* to her husband, she would, if the bill passed as it then was, be left destitute. The matter was arranged.

12. In Lord Bolingbroke's case (Lords' Journals, 26th February 1768), her ladyship acquiesced in the provision made for her by the bill, which thereon passed.

13. In the Duke of Grafton's case (Lords' Journals, 5th March 1769), the counsel for her grace said he was authorized to give her assent to the provision allowed to her by the bill.

14. In Mr. Dundas' case, Macq. H. of L. 614., the following remarkable clause had the sanction of Lords Eldon and Redesdale : "And the said annuity of 150*l.* shall be for the " separate and inalienable use of the said Jane Rollo Dundas, " and all obligations, contracts, agreements, or acts alienating " or tending to alienate the same, either in whole or in part, " shall be null and void to all intents and purposes whatso- " ever." This clause would operate whether the divorced wife afterwards married or continued single; so that it went beyond the separate use known in equity which exists only in the married state.

15. In the counter case, where the wife is the complainant, and prevails against her husband, it is more reasonable that she should have a provision; and it would seem that section thirty-two, as amended by the Commons, is sufficient, or meant to be sufficient, for the purpose.

16. It enacts, that on "*any*" divorce the court may order that the husband shall, to the satisfaction of the court, secure to the wife such gross sum of money, or such annual sum of money, for any term not exceeding her own life, as, having regard to her fortune, to the ability of her husband, and to the conduct of the parties, it shall deem reasonable, and for that purpose may refer it to one of the conveyancing counsel of the Court of Chancery to prepare a deed, &c.

17. The thirty-second section will thus have the sanction of the Code Napoleon, which lays it down that "the court " may award to the spouse obtaining the divorce, out of the " property of the other spouse, an alimentary allowance."

18. Suppose, therefore, the husband rich, but so profligate that the children cannot be left with him. Suppose the wife all that a wife should be. In such a case the court would give her the custody of the children, and order the husband to secure to her an allowance adequate for herself and for their maintenance and education, a result probably as beneficial as any that can arise under the act. See chapter xv., infra, p. 79.

19. The same section enacts, that in a suit for divorce "the
" court shall have the same power to make interim orders for
" payment to the wife, by way of alimony or otherwise, as it
" would have in a suit instituted for judicial separation."
And by section twenty-four it is enacted, that the court may
in all cases direct the alimony to be paid "either to the wife
" herself, or to any trustee on her behalf, to be approved by
" the court, and may impose any terms or restrictions which
" to the court may seem expedient, and may from time to
" time appoint a new trustee, if for any reason it shall appear
" to the court expedient so to do." The cases on alimony in
Doctors' Commons are not likely to govern the new jurisdiction
for this, amongst other reasons, that they are all without
reference to the children.

20. As there was an ecclesiastical and a parliamentary
liability on the husband to provide his wife with the means,
when necessary, of suing against him, or of resisting his
proceedings, so the new court will no doubt enforce a similar
obligation ; subject, however, it is to be hoped, to proper
guards and modifications ; otherwise the wife may fall into
hands not unwilling to distress the husband by exposure, or
to wear him out by expense. This has been the subject of
complaint in Scotland. A writer in the Journal of Jurisprudence, published at Edinburgh in April 1857, speaking of
divorce, says: "We have known cases where 800l. of ex-
" penses have been paid to the wife's agents, and where the
" husband has abandoned his action, and consented, during
" the remainder of his life, rather to give his wife a separate
" allowance."

CHAPTER XI.

OF JUDICIAL SEPARATION.

1. THE great jurist M. Portalis observes finely, that "mar-" riage does not subsist for the spouses alone, but for the " children, for society. It is in its esssence permanent. We " cannot prescribe a term to it."

2. Separation without the sanction of a judicial sentence is totally unknown to the Common Law of England. So says Mr. Roper. The countenance occasionally given to separations by private agreement was from the difficulty of obtaining them by judicial authority. When that difficulty disappears it will be found safer to insist on having the decision of a judge in every case, because in no other way can collusion and improper purposes be guarded against.

3. In Scotland private or voluntary separation does, indeed, take place occasionally, but it begets no legal obligation de futuro. It is treated by the judges with indulgence rather than with favour, and either party may put an end to it at

pleasure, the genius of Scotch law being all for durability in the married state.

4. In France there is no such thing recognized by law as separation without the sanction of a judge ; nor is it allowed in Sweden, or in Denmark, or in Holland, or in Prussia, or in Austria, or in Bavaria, or in Sardinia, or in the two Sicilies, or in the Canton de Vaud, or in Louisiana.

5. But, on the other hand, judicial separation, as contra-distinguished from voluntary, has been deemed a necessity in catholic and a convenience in protestant communities. It is accordingly retained by the Act "to amend the law relating "to divorce and matrimonial causes in England ;" although the head of the government, on the 6th of August last, de-clared that "the position in which man and wife were placed "by these judicial separations was most objectionable ; and if "marriage were dissolved at all, it should be dissolved alto-"gether. Judicial separation, therefore, ought to be the "exception, not the rule." So said Lord Palmerston. This was also Napoleon's view. See infra, p. 138.

6. Formerly judicial separation was known by the imposing title of divorce à mensâ et thoro ; but, for the sake of sim-plicity, and to mark it the more clearly from proper divorce, it is now and will be henceforth designated as judicial separation, liable, however, like divorce à mensâ et thoro, to be terminated by the reconciliation of the parties.

7. Judicial separation, however, is a great improvement upon divorce à mensâ et thoro.

8. In the first place, judicial separation may be granted by reason of desertion, a delinquency constantly overlooked in the ecclesiastical tribunals, sect. 16. Secondly, judicial sepa-ration will embrace the care of the children who, by the ecclesiastical tribunals, were left to their fate, sect. 35. Thirdly, judicial separation will bestow on the wife a new social status, giving her legal capabilities, and rendering her a feme sole as to after-acquired property, sect. 25 and 26.* And fourthly, arrangements may be made by the court on judicial separation which were never made on divorce à mensâ

* For this boon the women of England have to thank Lord Lyndhurst. After all, the law is but restored to what it was five centuries ago. See Lady Belknappe's case.—Lord Campbell's Lives of the Chief Justices, vol. 1, p. 113, and vol. 3, p. 47. See also infra, p. 122.

et thoro,—arrangements which will not fall to the ground on renewal of cohabitation, sect. 25.

9. Applications for judicial separation will be "heard and " determined by the judge ordinary, either alone or with one " or more of the other judges of the said court," sect. 9.

10. No decree shall hereafter be made for divorce à mensâ et thoro, but instead thereof, the court may pronounce a decree for a judicial separation, sect. 7.

11. A sentence of judicial separation may be obtained, either by the husband or the wife, on the ground of adultery, or cruelty, or desertion without cause for two years and upwards, sect. 16.

12. Application for judicial separation may be made, by either husband or wife, by petition to the court ; and the court, on being satisfied of the truth of the allegations therein contained, and that there is no legal ground why the same should not be granted, may decree such judicial separation accordingly ; and, where the application is by the wife, may make any order for alimony which shall be deemed just, sect. 17. See chapter x.

13. Any husband may in his petition for judicial separation claim damages from the adulterer, sect. 33. For the proceedings upon such a claim, see chapter XIII.

14. Every person seeking a decree of judicial separation shall, together with the petition or other application for the same, file an affidavit verifying the same, so far as he or she is able to do so, and stating that there is not any collusion or connivance between the deponent and the other party to the marriage, sect. 41. See supra, p. 39.

15. It shall be lawful for, but not obligatory upon, the court to direct questions of fact to be determined before itself, or any one or more of the judges of the said court, by the verdict of a special or common jury, sect. 36.

16. The court, if it think fit, may order the attendance of the petitioner for examination, sect. 43.

17. The court may make such interim orders, and in its final decree such provision as it may deem proper with respect to the custody, maintenance, and education of the children ; and, if it shall think fit, may direct proceedings to be taken for placing such children under the protection of the Court of Chancery, sect. 35. See chapter xv.

18. In all cases in which the court shall make any decree or order for alimony, it may direct the same to be paid either to the wife herself, or to any trustee on her behalf to be approved by the court, and may impose any terms and restrictions which to the court may seem expedient, and may from time to time appoint a new trustee, if for any reason it shall appear to the court expedient so to do, sect. 24. See chapter X.

19. If, on judicial separation for the wife's adultery, it shall appear that she is entitled to any property either in possession or reversion, it shall be lawful for the court to order such settlement as it shall think reasonable to be made of such property, or any part thereof, for the benefit of the innocent party, and of the children of the marriage, or either or any of them, Sect 45. See chapter XII.

20. The wife shall, from the date of the sentence and whilst the separation continues, be considered a feme sole with respect to any property she may acquire, or which may come to or devolve upon her; provided, that if she shall again cohabit with her husband, all such property as she may be entitled to when such cohabitation shall take place, shall be held to her separate use, subject, however, to any agreement in writing made between herself and her husband whilst separate, sect. 25.

21. The wife shall, whilst separate, be considered a feme sole for the purposes of contract, wrongs, and injuries, and for the purposes of suing and being sued in any civil proceeding, and her husband shall not be liable in respect of any engagement or contract she may have entered into, provided that where alimony has been ordered to be paid to her, and the same shall not be duly paid by the husband, he shall be liable for necessaries supplied for her use; and provided also, that nothing shall prevent the wife from joining, at any time during such separation, in the exercise of any joint power given to herself and her husband, sect. 26.

22. It is remarkable, that by these two sections (25 and 26 of the Act) the immunities and powers given to the wife are irrespective of the question, whether the sentence is to be for her husband's delinquency or her own, and irrespective of the other question, whether there are children or not of the marriage. In this way a culpable wife judicially separated

gets rid of the encumbrance of a husband, leaves her children on *his* hands, and sets up independently on her own account. The question is, whether it would not have been better to legislate for the benefit of the deserving injured wife, she living chastely under judicial separation, and thus hold out no bonus or reward to the delinquent one, who, on the contrary, ought to be compelled, if able, to contribute towards the rearing and education of the children, supposing the husband to be without adequate means for that purpose.

23. Mr. Justice Blackstone, 1 Comm. 456, tells us, that "if, " after divorce à mensâ et thoro, the wife breeds children, " they are bastards, for the law will presume that the hus- " band and wife conform to the sentence unless access is " proved." The like result will, it is presumed, arise under the 20 & 21 Vict. c. 85., section 7 enacting that a decree for judicial separation shall have the same force and the same consequences as a divorce à mensâ et thoro.

24. Either party may at any time after a decree of separation present a petition, praying that such decree be reversed " on the ground that it was obtained in his or her absence, " and that there was reasonable ground for the alleged deser- " tion where desertion was the ground of such decree;" and the court may, on being satisfied of the truth of the allegations, reverse its own decree accordingly, but the reversal shall not affect the rights of third parties, sect. 23. This seems to be on the principle of a bill of review in equity combined with the fact superadded, that the decision sought to be reversed was pronounced behind the back of the defendant.

25. Either party, dissatisfied with any decision of the judge ordinary alone, may, within three calendar months after the pronouncing thereof, appeal therefrom to the full court, whose decision shall be final, sect. 55. But what if the decision is by the Judge Ordinary, "with one or more of the other judges ?" Sect. 9.

26. The court shall give relief on principles and rules which, in its opinion, shall be as nearly as may be conformable to the principles and rules on which the ecclesiastical courts have heretofore acted and given relief, but subject to the provisions herein contained, and to the rules and orders under this act, sect. 22.

27. On the 18th of August last the Attorney General, with reference to the practice of the ecclesiastical tribunals, which he pronounced " extremely anomalous," observed that " as the " bill was worded, it would not throw on the new court the " obligation of adopting that practice on judicial separation ; " and it was matter for grave consideration whether it " was a desirable thing to retain." On the 21st of August Mr. Henley said " the ecclesiastical rules were no longer to " govern."

28. As an example of the "anomalies" doubtless in the mind of the learned Attorney General, we may mention a curious condition imposed by the ecclesiastical courts on all applicants for divorce à mensâ et thoro. It appears that in the year 1597 the Chamber of Convocation passed a canon which requires that " in all sentences pronounced for divorce à " mensâ et thoro there shall be a restraint inserted that the " parties shall live chastely, and that they shall not contract " matrimony with other persons." In compliance with this mandate the ecclesiastical courts have ever since exacted a pecuniary bond with two sureties for celibacy on the part of suitors seeking judicial separation. If the wife is complainant, she must not only get two sureties, but provide a man to execute the bond in her stead ; and, unless the new court interfere by an order of abolition, we must still retain a species of duresse for which it will not be easy to find a parallel in any department of any jurisprudence in the world.

The prohibitory bond, however, is imposed as a condition on the party seeking the remedy, the court having no power over the respondent. The stipulation for chastity is omitted.

Thus a canon absurd in itself is rendered more absurd by being made to point at one only of the parties, while its authors plainly intended it to operate equally against both, though what good purpose, even if fully carried out, it was likely to serve, it will require some ingenuity to discover.

29. BARS TO JUDICIAL SEPARATION.

If divorce is to be the rule, and judicial separation the exception, the bars to judicial separation will hardly be fewer than the bars to divorce. The statute is not explicit here, section 17 merely saying that " the court on being satisfied of " the truth of the allegations, and that there is no legal

F

" ground why the same should not be granted," may decree judicial separation.

The bars to divorce are stated supra, chapter VII., p. 42.

In the case of young couples, separations, whether judicial or voluntary, must be perilous to both parties. But where middle life is arrived at or past, and where, moreover, there are children of the marriage, divorce should be reluctantly conceded; while, on the other hand, judicial separation may very fitly answer all that can be reasonably desired.

30. And here it will be regretted that the suggestion of a great person was allowed to fall to the ground. The Marquis of Lansdowne in March last recommended that in cases where reconciliation was possible, although the proofs of delinquency might be sufficient, yet the court should not at once pronounce sentence, but postpone it for a period in conformity with the French practice, infra p. 132. Lord Lansdowne said that the best effects were found to flow from this locus pœnitentiæ, which not only afforded leisure for reflection, but gave friends an opportunity to interpose. It is true, however, that the remark applies rather to divorce than to judicial separation. When the injury is of such a kind that forgiveness may be hoped for, a pause before making the decree may be highly expedient. But for this there seems no authority in the Act.

31. Again, it may be remarked, that section 3 enables the new Court " to enforce " or " otherwise deal with " any decree or order of any ecclesiastical court made prior to the passing of the Act, precisely as if such decree or order had been made originally by the new jurisdiction itself. Therefore, an appeal will lie from Sir John Dodson or Dr. Lushington, if within time, to the full court, just as if the Judge Ordinary had made the decree. Such appears to be the intention.

CHAPTER XII.

POWER ON DIVORCE OR JUDICIAL SEPARATION TO ORDER A SETTLEMENT OF THE DELINQUENT WIFE'S PROPERTY.

1. A CLAUSE not occurring in the bills of 1854 and 1856, and placed in an odd part of the recent act, namely, section forty-five, enacts, that in any case of divorce or judicial separation "for adultery of the wife," if it appear that she is entitled to any property in possession or reversion, the court, "if it " shall think proper," shall order such settlement "as it shall " think reasonable" to be made of such property, or any part thereof, "for the benefit of the innocent party and of the " children of the marriage, or either or any of them."

2. This in principle seems to follow the wise and good law of Napoleon.

3. When the wife has property in reversion, the Act of the late Session, 20 & 21 Vict. c. 57. will be kept in view.

4. When the wife has property limited to her separate use, in the equitable sense of the phrase, she is not bound to contribute to family purposes, whether living with or apart from her husband. The court, on divorce or judicial separation, may, to a certain extent, correct this evil under the above clause.

5. Parliament, when it chose, rescinded or moulded existing settlements; but unfortunately the court cannot do so; and cases will soon arise in which the want of this power will be regretted.

6. With respect to the wife's property *not* limited to her separate use, we have seen, supra p. 47, that the act has nowhere defined the effects of divorce. Consequently, where

divorce is granted, difficulties or doubts may arise in directing and preparing the settlement; because, before putting anything in settlement as appertaining to the wife, it ought clearly to appear how far her property is, or is not, affected by the operation of the mere sentence dissolving the marriage; in other words, what is the general legal consequence of a divorce as regards the property of the parties.

6. Suppose the husband to be tenant by the curtesy initiate. Suppose him likewise to be the "innocent party" under section 45. If, on divorce, he becomes tenant by the curtesy consummate, and if he be entitled "to the rents of " his wife's lands as if she were naturally dead" (the rule in Scotland, Professor More informs us, supra p. 57), the court cannot deprive him of such legal right; but if it order a settlement, it will be one very different from that which would be directed in the husband's favour, supposing him *not* entitled to the curtesy.

7. The court, if it think proper, shall direct a settlement, not only in cases of divorce, but in cases of judicial separation. It appears that the words " or judicial separation" were added by the Commons.

CHAPTER XIII.

HUSBAND'S CLAIM OF DAMAGES FROM THE SEDUCER OF HIS WIFE; EITHER AS INCIDENT TO DIVORCE OR JUDICIAL SEPARATION, OR AS AN INDEPENDENT PROCEEDING.

1. AFTER the 20 & 21 Vict. c. 85. shall have come into operation no action shall be maintainable in England for criminal conversation; sect. 59.

2. But the same statute which thus abolishes the action, substitutes another proceeding, not very dissimilar.

3. Thus section thirty-three, introduced by the Commons enacts, that "any husband may, either in a petition for dis-" solution of marriage, or for judicial separation, *or in a peti-*" *tion limited to such object only,* claim damages from any " person on the ground of his having committed adultery with " the wife of such petitioner."

4. What is meant by a petition "limited to such object only" is not clear. Perhaps the petitioner is to be at liberty to ask damages without asking divorce or judicial separation.

5. The petition must be served on the alleged adulterer, and also on the alleged adulteress, unless the court shall dispense with such service, or direct some other.

6. The claim for damages "shall be heard and tried on the same principles, in the same manner, and subject to the like rules and regulations as actions for criminal conversation are

now tried and decided in Courts of Common Law." Here the meaning is plain enough.

7. The same section thirty-three, after enacting that the other provisions of the act as to the hearing and decision of petitions shall, as far as possible, be deemed applicable to the hearing and decision of petitions for damages, enacts that the damages "shall in all cases be ascertained by the verdict of a jury, although the respondents, or either of them, may not appear."

8. Finally, by this section the court is to direct the payment and application of the damages; and may order that the whole, or any part thereof, shall be "settled" for the benefit of the petitioner's children, or as a provision for their delinquent mother. The court, it is presumed, will be slow to do this, remembering what Lord St. Leonards said on the return of the bill to the Lords.* It is new to render the wife's shame a source of permanent subsistence for her children and herself, under the superintendence of a tribunal expressly appointed to guard and advance the morals of the country.

9. Sometimes the wife may think more of her pecuniary interest than of her character, because the larger the damages the better the settlement. She may, therefore, collude with her husband.

10. It was said by Mr. Henley, that, notwithstanding the indignation expressed against crim. con. actions, the legislature had retained them in substance by this singular section.

11. But although the remark of Mr. Henley is just, there are reasons for hoping that the section itself will prove in most cases a dead letter. In the first place, a proceeding for damages against the adulterer will be no longer, as heretofore, an indispensable preliminary to divorce; secondly, such a proceeding will be under the jealous eye, if not the frown, of the court and the jury; and, thirdly, the plaintiffs, even though successful, will have no certainty of deriving any direct pecuniary benefit from the application.

---

* "The clause that the damages might be settled for the benefit of the children was monstrous. He (Lord St. Leonards) would rather touch a scorpion than the money awarded in compensation of dishonour."—25th August 1857.

12. Suppose, however, that the wife, by industry and talent, actually maintains her husband. The seduction of such a valuable wife would be an injury more than sentimental ; and might be thought a very fit ground for pecuniary compensation which the court ought to be empowered to award without a jury. This, however, section thirty-three seems to forbid.

13. Lord Granville, on the 25th August last, mentioned, in his place the case of a professional man of 400*l.* a year, having a wife of 1,200*l.* a year. She eloped, leaving six daughters on the hands of her ill-starred husband. His lordship thought that for such an injury it was reasonable that a man should "be able" to sue the seducer for damages.

14. After the printing of the preceding chapter, there appeared the "Handy Book" of Lord St. Leonards, from which I take the liberty of quoting the following striking passage * :—"The action of crim. con., that disgrace to the
" nation, has been abolished ; but, by an unpardonable mis-
" take in legislation, this is accomplished in words only,
" whilst in effect, indeed in words equally plain, a similar
" right of action is given to the husband through the instru-
" mentality of the Court, but to be tried by a jury. A man
" may now recover damages for his wife's infidelity without
" seeking for a divorce, but may continue to live with her
" upon the damages recovered from the paramour, which may
" be settled upon her and upon the children. Even when a
" divorce is obtained, the damages may be settled upon the
" children of the marriage; and the father may live with his
" children whilst they are maintained and educated with the
" price of their mother's dishonour."

---

* p. 77.

CHAPTER XIV.

SUITS OF NULLITY.

---

1. IN the Roman Catholic ages, suits to nullify marriages furnished the spiritual courts with their staple occupation.

2. The process of declaring a marriage null was curiously called divorce à vinculo matrimonii. The reason of this designation, though not satisfactory, was intelligible, for the canonists often, under the pretence of annulling, really dissolved the matrimonial tie. On the payment of moderate fees they were able in almost every case to make out that any marriage was void ab initio, or, at all events, voidable. The learned commissioners explain how this was done in their Report, p. 3.

3. Thus, we are informed, that the number of impediments to matrimony was increased by extending to the eighth degree the legal prohibitions of consanguinity and affinity.

4. Another device was, to declare that a relationship might be contracted by mere commerce between the sexes. Thus, if

a man had carnally known one sister, it was held incestuous in him to marry or have sexual intercourse with the other sister. The Scotch, the most Protestant people in Europe, retain still much of the canon law in their matrimonial code. On the 2d August 1628 George Sinclair was criminally convicted on the ground that he had had intercourse with two sisters, though married to neither; he had sentence to be drowned. And on the 2d June 1643 Janet Imbril was found guilty of "keeping company" with John and Andrew Thomson, two brothers, though she was the wife of neither. The court condemned her to be beheaded. (1 Hume's Crim. Law of Scotland, 446.) Fornication, therefore, according to these authorities, was as much the cause of affinity as matrimony itself. To cite a higher illustration:—Margaret, daughter of Henry 7th and widow of James 4th, having after the Scotch king's death intermarried with Lord Methven, succeeded in getting rid of him by a sentence of the ecclesiastical court at St. Andrew's, by showing that she had been, as the record expressed it, carnaliter cognita by her husband's fourth cousin, the Earl of Angus.

5. But the old ecclesiastical law of this country went beyond all this, for Lord Coke tells us that "there was a time "in England when divorce à vinculo matrimonii might be "had because the husband had stood godfather to his wife's "cousin."

6. A previous betrothment was another impediment to matrimony. It was not by the axe that the promoter of the English Reformation extinguished his marriage with Anne Boleyne. He first carried her into the ecclesiastical court, and there obtained a sentence on the ground of her alleged precontract with Northumberland.

7. Everyone knows how much it was the policy of the Roman church to multiply these impediments, the granting of dispensations having been in all ages a favourite exercise of papal authority, and a fruitful source of ecclesiastical revenue.

8. When, however, the Reformation came, canonical impediments, except such as had the sanction of Scripture, were each and all put an end to by the 32 Henry 8. c. 38. This was a deep blow to suits of nullity.

9. They sustained a further discouragement within our own recollection. To understand this we must observe, that anciently a well-known legal distinction existed between marriages absolutely void and marriages simply voidable.

10. " A voidable marriage, if not annulled during the life-
" time of the parties who had contracted it, could never
" afterwards be impeached. If either of the parties died
" during the pendency of proceedings and before sentence,
" the marriage remained valid, and the legitimacy of the off-
" spring was fully and conclusively established. From this
" state of the law hardships and disasters often arose. The
" legitimacy of the children might remain in suspense more
" than half a century ; parties might marry and have children
" born to them ; the eldest son might come to the age of
" twenty-five, and, on the supposition that as no proceedings
" had ever been taken, he was legitimate, and as such was
" entitled to succeed to his father's property, he might
" marry ; he might have children ; and between ten and
" fifteen years afterwards there might be a suit in the Eccle-
" siastical Court ; he might be bastardized, and his children
" deprived of the means and the hopes of that fortune which
" they had been accustomed to consider as their own."*

11. To remedy these evils Lord Lyndhurst brought in a bill
the 5 & 6 Will. 4. c. 54., enacting that all marriages celebrated
before the 31st August 1835 " between persons being within
" the prohibited degrees of affinity should not thereafter be
" annulled, for that cause, by any sentence of the Ecclesias-
" tical Court, provided that nothing therein enacted should
" affect marriages between parties being within the prohibited
" degrees of consanguinity." The second section enacted that
" all marriages which should thereafter be celebrated between
" persons within the prohibited degrees of consanguinity or
" affinity should be absolutely null and void to all intents
" and purposes whatsoever." Then followed a proviso excluding Scotland from the operation of the statute.

12. The act does not touch upon the question what shall
or what shall not be included under the head of prohibited
degrees.

---

* Per Lord Lyndhurst, 1 June 1835.

· 13. It was considered that many persons might be disposed to run the risk of a voidable marriage, but that few, or none, would knowingly enter into a marriage that was by law absolutely void. ·The measure excited less attention at the time than it has done since.

14. The result is, that since the passing of Lord Lyndhurst's act all marriages within the prohibited degrees, whether of consanguinity or affinity, are, ipso facto, absolutely void; and suits of nullity on the ground of the prohibited degrees, are now few and far between.

15. One vexed question still remains, as to marrying the deceased wife's sister, by making a run to a country where such marriage is allowed. But the opinion delivered by Mr. Justice Cresswell, in Brooke v. Brooke, on the 4th Dec. 1857, has gone far to determine it. See Weekly Rep., 12th Dec. 1857. The learned judge held that the marriage in Brooke v. Brooke was void.

16. It has been decided that consanguinity and affinity are impediments to matrimony, whether the relationship be legitimate or illegitimate. (Horner v. Horner, 1 Con. 353.)

17. We have seen, supra p. 10, that under 4 Geo. 4. c. 76 the penalty of nullity was confined to the knowingly proceeding with the celebration in the face of circumstances implying a wilful disobedience of the statute by both parties. In Wright v. Elwood, 1 Curt. 49, Dr. Lushington held that the marriage was not void where only one of the parties knew of the undue publication of banns.

18. When a marriage was challenged on the score of corporal incapacity, the Court Spiritual put the matter in a train of investigation.

The defect might be in either of the parties; for, says Oughton, "Impedimentum contingat tam in muliere quam in " viro."

19. The method of inquiry is described by Oughton in his Ordo, p. 320, under the following heads, which he entitles,—

DE MODO PROBANDI DEFECTUS INTER CONJUGATOS.

Modus inspectionis viri.

Juramentum de fideliter inspiciando. Forma relationis judicii medicorum quod defectus in viro sit insanibilis.

Forma allegationis ea propter ex parte mulieris. Quid si relatio de viro sit dubia ?

Modus inspectionis mulieris.

Defectus in muliere inspiciat obstetrices. Harum juramentum. Relatio judicii. Quid si relatio de muliere sit dubia ? See also Ayliffe's Parergon, 227.

20. To give cases in this branch of jurisdiction would not edify. It has been thought that the mode of investigation is unsatisfactory and deceptive. This seems very likely. Take Bury's case (5 Rep. 98, Dyer 179). He was charged by his wife with impotency. The marriage was held null. He married again, *and had issue !* Handfuls of similar examples may be found. Sometimes a wrong person was submitted to inspection.

The new court will take order in this matter.

21. We proceed to the third ground of nullity, namely, insanity of the mind, involving an incapacity to contract. When this occurs on either side, there is no marriage.

22. Every case of this sort must be one of circumstances.

23. The want or failure of reason may arise from idiotcy or lunacy. The learning applicable to such an inquiry has recently been expanded and matured. A statement of it here would be beyond the scope of this commentary. The ecclesiastical authorities will be deemed of less importance, seeing that the new court will in all probability devolve the investigation upon juries.

24. In Turner v. Meyers, (1 Hagg. Con. 416), a husband having recovered from his insanity was allowed to prosecute a suit of nullity on the ground that at the time of the marriage he was not in a state of mind competent to contract. Dealing with this singular application, Sir William Scott said, " It is perfectly clear in law that a party may come forward " to maintain his own *past* incapacity." Turner was a Lincolnshire grazier, whom the Court held capable of estimating the aberrations of his own understanding.

25. Another ground of nullity is *force* or *fear*. As an illustration of this article, the Rape of the Sabines is gravely cited. More relevant is the case of Miss Anne Leigh and of the ill-used " gentlewoman," both mentioned supra, p. 3.

26. Ayliffe tells us that the effect of this impediment, force or fear, may be done away with by a subsequent spontaneous cohabitation'; and Dr. Taylor * holds that the Sabines ought to have the benefit of this construction. We see no objection.

27. There may be nullity on the score of error. "Canonically " there are four sorts of error :—1st, *Error Personæ ;* as when " *A.,* intending to marry Elizabeth, through mistake marries " Jane." Under the head of Error Personæ, Beau Fielding's case may perhaps be ranged; supra p. 4. If so, the decision was wrong. "2dly, there may be *Error Conditionis ;* a case " entirely obsolete ; as, if *A.* marries *B.,* thinking her to be a " free woman, when, in reality, she is a slave. 3dly, *Error* " *Fortunæ ;* when a man, expecting to marry a rich wife, after- " wards discovers her to be a poor one. And, 4thly, *Error* " *Qualitatis ;* when one party is mistaken in the rank or " quality of the other ; or, when a man, thinking to marry a " chaste woman, discovers her to be of the opposite character." See Mr. Poynter's compendious book on the practice of Doctors Commons, published in 1824.

28. Bigamy.—It seems scarcely necessary to say that a prior marriage, if it be valid, will render a second one —living the parties—good for nothing. See Beau Fielding's case, supra p. 4.

The having two wives, or two husbands, at the same time, is a criminal offence, and therefore the cognizance of such cases belongs to criminal jurisprudence ; though a suit of nullity might no doubt still be sustained, supposing parties desirous of trying the experiment.

29. Under the act all applications for sentences of nullity shall be by petition ; which shall be heard and determined by three or more judges of the said court, of whom the judge of the Court of Probate shall be one ; Sect. 10.

30. It may be asked, who shall be petitioner in such a case ? Neither of the parties is likely to move. In Ray *v.* Sherwood the suit of nullity was by the father of the wife. It was insisted that he had no interest sufficient to enable him to sustain the proceeding. But the Judicial Committee of Privy Council determined otherwise, and the marriage was held null. It would seem that any interest, however slight, provided it be

* Elements of Civil Law.

specific and pecuniary, whether to be secured in a contingent right, or released from a possible legal obligation, will entitle a party to sustain a suit for nullity by reason of the prohibited degrees. Sherwood *v.* Ray, 1 Moore, P. C. Ca., 353.

31. Every person seeking a decree of nullity of marriage shall, together with the petition or other application for the same, file an affidavit verifying the same, so far as he or she is able to do so; and stating that there is not any collusion or connivance between the deponent and the other party to the marriage.— Sect. 41. This assumes that every application for nullity is to be by the husband or by the wife, whereas it is not likely to be by either.

32. It shall be lawful for, but not obligatory upon, the court to direct questions of fact to be determined before itself, or any one or more of the judges of the said court, by the verdict of a special or common jury.—Sect. 36.

33. The court, if it shall think fit, may order the attendance of the petitioner for examination.—Sect. 43.

34. The court may make such interim orders, and in its final decree such provision, as it may deem proper with respect to the custody, maintenance, and education of the children; and, if it shall think fit, may direct proceedings to be taken for placing such children under the protection of the Court of Chancery.— Sect. 35. See the next chapter.

35. When a sentence of nullity is pronounced, the children are ipso facto illegitimate. As such they will have no property. And, even if there was a settlement on the occasion of the false nuptials, such settlement it is presumed must wholly fail.

36. The court shall give relief in accordance with ecclesiastical principles, but subject to the provisions of the act, and to the rules and orders to be made in pursuance thereof.

37. Suits of nullity must be heard and determined by what sect. 55. calls the "full court." Sect. 56. gives an appeal to the House of Lords, where "either party is dissatisfied with " the decision of the full court on any petition for the dissolu- " tion of marriage." But it does not appear that any appeal is given on a decree for nullity of marriage.

CHAPTER XV.

CUSTODY, MAINTENANCE, AND EDUCATION OF THE CHILDREN.

---

1. WITH respect to the custody, maintenance, and education of the children in cases of divorce, cases of judicial separation, and cases of nullity, the court is empowered by the Act to make such interim orders and such ultimate provision as it may deem just and proper; Sect. 35.

2. This latitude of discretion will enable the court to consult not only its own wisdom, but the practice and experience of other countries.

3. By the Code Napoleon, the custody, pendente lite, in cases of divorce, is to remain with the father, whether demandant or defendant, till the court shall otherwise order. Code Napoleon, Art. 35, infra, p. 138.

4. This seems also to be the rule in Scotland, and it will probably be the rule of the new court.

5. Of the ultimate custody when divorce is pronounced, the Roman law says, "Divortio facto, Judex æstimabit utrum apud patrem, an apud matrem, filii morari ac nutriri debeant." Cod. 5, tit. 24. According to this, the court must consider and decide, whether asked to do so or not.

6. By the Code Napoleon, Art. 50, infra, p. 134, the ultimate custody when divorce is pronounced shall be confided to the spouse who has obtained the divorce, unless the court, on the application of the family or of the public officer, shall order, for the greater advantage of the children, that all or some of them be committed to the care of the other spouse or of a third party. Here the ultimate custody follows the decree, unless on special grounds the court order otherwise.

7. In Scotland the paternal right is not displaced by the decree of divorce, the Scotch law holding that conjugal misconduct does not of itself necessarily imply absolute unfitness for the care of the children.

8. The new court may act ex proprio motu, or wait till it is applied to. It may hold, with the Code Napoleon, that the custody shall, as a general rule, follow the decree, subject to exceptional modification; or it may subscribe to the Scotch practice which is, to leave undisturbed the paternal authority, unless some special ground be stated and established for controlling it.

9. Where the husband obtains the divorce, his legal authority over the children will of course be continued in him. Therefore it is, in truth, only where the wife is complainant that this jurisdiction is likely to be exercised.

10. The grounds of its exercise will probably be the same as the grounds on which the Court of Chancery proceeds, when it supersedes the patria protestas; with this difference, that the Divorce Court will always have before it two parties, of whom one is likely to be meritorious; whereas the Court of Chancery is often obliged to give the custody to strangers; as, for example, in Allen v. Coster, 1 Beav. 202, where both parents were bad; and in the Wellesley case, where, the mother being dead, and the father profligate, the children were taken from him. It is evidently a less strong thing to commit the

custody to the wife who has obtained the divorce, than to any third party.

11. The cases in which the Court of Chancery interferes are generally where the interests of the children render it a necessity that the father's power over them be suspended, or abrogated; as where he inculcates irreligion or immorality by precept or example; where he is an habitual incorrigible drunkard; where he systematically retards or neglects his children's education; where he treats them with harshness and cruelty; where he dissipates their means, or is wanting in the due care of it; or even where he is in such pecuniary circumstances as make it hazardous to leave him in the charge of their property: in each and all of these cases the legal right of the father will be displaced, supposing the attendant circumstances to be such as will enable the court to act with advantage and with effect.*

12. The aggravated cases entitling the wife to demand divorce under the Act are cases which, when made out against the husband, will, without more, go far to remove him from the custody of his children. Thus, first, where the husband is guilty of incestuous adultery within the meaning of section 27, we have a precedent for his supersession in Mrs. Addison's case (Macq., H. of L., 598). There the Act of divorce contained the following clause :—" And in order to secure, as far " as circumstances will admit, the virtuous education of the " children of the said marriage, be it declared and enacted, " that it shall not be lawful for the said Edward Addison to " remove his daughter from the care and custody of her " mother during her minority; and that the son and daughter " of the said Edward Addison shall during their respective " minorities be deemed and taken to be to all intents and " purposes wards of the Court of Chancery." This clause had the sanction of Lord Thurlow, Lord Chancellor Loughborough, and Lord Eldon.

13. Let us next consider the case of a husband guilty of " bigamy with adultery " within the meaning of section 27. Although we have no precedent here, it may safely be affirmed that the collateral circumstances must indeed be strong that will induce the court to leave with such a husband the custody

---

* See Mr. Tudor's excellent collection of authorities on this subject, and his valuable commentaries, 2 Tudor's Leading Ca. Eq. p. 563, 2nd Ed.

of the children; especially if the connexion with the second wife be maintained.

14. What shall be the effect on the children when the husband is divorced for having committed a rape? This, indeed, is a delinquency of deep depravity; but whether in all cases it necessarily disqualifies the father from taking care of his children the court will decide.

15. As to unnatural offences, the ruling precedent will be that made by Lord Cranworth when Vice Chancellor in the anonymous case reported 2 Sim., N. S. 54. The marginal note thus sums up the result:—" The court will refuse to give posses-
" sion of children to their father if he has so conducted himself,
" as that it will not be for the benefit of the infants, or if it
" will affect their happiness, or if they cannot associate with him
" without moral contamination, or if, because they associate
" with him, others will shun their society. If it be established
" to the satisfaction of the court that the father of children
" from ten to two years of age is to be considered as guilty of
" the perpetration of an unnatural crime, it is impossible to
" permit any sort of intercourse with his children even after
" he has escaped conviction. Semble that under such circum-
" stances, if the children were with their father, it would be
" the duty of the court to remove them."

16. To proceed in the order of the Act, take the case where the wife obtains divorce against her husband for "adultery with cruelty" within the meaning of the 27th section. Here, if the cruelty extend to the children, the custody will probably be changed.

17. Lastly, shall the husband be deprived of the custody where the wife obtains divorce against him for "adultery coupled with desertion" within the meaning of the 27th section? Cases have occurred where adultery and desertion were both attributable to a husband not wanting in affection for his children and attention to their interests.

18. Suppose the court gives the custody to the wife obtaining the divorce, and she remarries. Shall the custody continue? Can the court interfere again when the suit is at an end?

19. As to the custody in cases of judicial separation, the French jurist Zacharie lays it down, " 1. That the father who
" has obtained the separatson de corps can never be deprived

" of the custody of the children.   2. That that custody may
" be confided to the father against whom separation de corps
" has been pronounced." But, subject to these qualifications,
the French judges, having a large discretion, may, he holds,
give the custody to the mother, or to a third party. The
father's power, then, is not absolutely displaced by separation
de corps, as it is by divorce. Another French writer, M. Demolombe, affirms, that the paternal authority is to be continued
on separation de corps even when obtained against the father,
unless the court, by an express order, remove the children.
But, after a reviewal of the authorities, he arrives at this
conclusion, that the whole matter is in the discretion of the
court, having regard to the interests of the children, his
expression being, " Les Tribunaux aviseraient, suivant les
" cas, pour le plus grand avantage des enfants."

20. In every case where the wife can sustain a petition for
divorce she may restrict her demand to judicial separation.
When she does so, the question as to the children will, I
apprehend, be pretty much the same as if she had asked for
divorce, because, under judicial separation, a wife holds a
position qualifying her to take charge of the children almost
as effectively as if she had succeeded in obtaining a divorce.

21. Where the wife obtains a judicial separation on the
ground of adultery, she will not be likely to obtain the custody of the children. The discretion of the court, however, is
large.

22. Where she gets a judicial separation on the ground
of cruelty, the question will be whether the cruelty extends
to the children; for, if it do, the paternal power must give
way.

23. Where the wife obtains judicial separation on the
ground of desertion, it may happen that the desertion is
confined to herself, and is not unaccompanied with a sufficient
paternal care of the children. In such case the father will
retain his dominion.

24. The court, upon a view of all the circumstances, will
decide what is best for the maintenance and education of the
children, these being the sole objects of its interposition in the
exercise of this critical department of the jurisdiction conferred
by the statute.

25. And here it seems scarcely necessary to observe, that there must be property to enable the court to act; for, as Lord Eldon said in the Wellesley case, "the court cannot "take on itself the maintenance of all the children in the "kingdom." The property may belong to the children, or may be secured for their benefit by a third party; and when the father waives his paternal right in favour of such third party, such waiver will be enforced.

26. But all arrangements of property must be subservient to higher interests—"the virtuous education of the children," to use the language of the clause in Mrs. Addison's case, being the first object, compared with which all other considerations are secondary.

27. When the Court of Chancery separates the child from the father it takes care that the separation shall not have a greater effect than the case requires. "It is important," said Lord Cottenham, "that the faults of either parent should be "as far as possible concealed from the children, who should "be allowed the chance of being brought up with a good "opinion of both." It is wrong, therefore, to exclude even an erring parent from all intercourse with the offspring. (Macq. on Husband and Wife, 354.) Not only in the case of divorce, but in the case of judicial separation, there will be difficulty in carrying these views into effect; but here will be an opportunity for the new court to display its wisdom.

28. Finally, it will be asked, whose shall the custody of the children be when the marriage is judicially ascertained to be null and void? This the court will determine when called upon to do so, which will not be often.

29. Cases may arise in which it will be expedient to invoke the aid of the Court of Chancery. Hence section 35 enacts that reference may be had, when necessary, to the energies of that high tribunal. But why was not power given to the new Court to do its own business?

CHAPTER XVI.

RESTITUTION OF CONJUGAL RIGHTS.

1. WHY is this strange, inaccurate, tedious title retained? The court may enforce duties, but to restore lost rights is beyond its power. Besides, there are some conjugal rights which belong to a different jurisdiction; yet here is an affectation of a general restitution.

2. When Mrs. Dalrymple followed her husband to this country, supra p. 13, her suit was for "restitution of conjugal rights;" and when Sir William Scott pronounced judgment in her favour, he ordered Mr. Dalrymple "to receive her " home as his wife, and treat her with conjugal affection." This corresponds with the Scottish sentence of " adherence."

3. In suits for restitution of conjugal rights the complaint is, that the respondent has, without lawful cause, withdrawn from cohabitation.

4. In Scotland, by serving the judicial requisition of " adherence," the ground, after a certain period of contumacy, is laid for the further proceeding of divorce by reason of desertion. The suit for restitution of conjugal rights is really a suit for desertion; but the redress it affords is inadequate, and therefore few apply for it.

5. The respondent may deny the marriage. The case will then assume the character of a suit for nullity.—Swift v. Swift, 4 Hagg. 153.

6. Where the plea of adultery or the plea of cruelty was proved, the defendant became entitled to divorce à mensâ et thoro.—Best *v.* Best, 1 Add. 412.

7. Although the defendant sought merely a dismissal of the suit for restitution of conjugal rights, the court was in the habit, on proof of adultery or cruelty, of pronouncing ex proprio motu a sentence of divorce à mensâ et thoro.—1 Macq. Rep. 257.

8. But this was surely wrong, since it is well settled that both divorce and judicial separation are private remedies, to be granted only when demanded by the party injured.

9. Suits for restitution of conjugal rights are under the act " to be heard and determined by the judge ordinary alone, or " with one or more of the other judges of the said court ;" sect. 9.

10. Applications for restitution of conjugal rights may be made either by husband or wife by petition to the court ; and the court, on being satisfied of the truth of the allegations therein contained, and that there is no legal ground why the same should not be granted, may decree such restitution of conjugal rights accordingly ; sect. 17.

11. It shall be lawful for, but not obligatory upon, the court to direct questions of fact to be determined by the verdict of a special or a common jury, either before the court itself, or before any one, or more, of the judges of the said courts, sect. 36.

12. The court may, if it shall think fit, order the attendance of the petitioner, and may examine him or her, or permit him or her to be examined or cross-examined on oath on the hearing of any such petition ; but no such petitioner shall be bound to answer any question tending to shew that he or she has been guilty of adultery, sect. 43.

13. The court shall act and give relief on principles similar to those which have hitherto governed the ecclesiastical courts, subject, however, to the provisions of the act, and to the rules and orders under the act ; sect. 22.

14. Adultery and cruelty were respectively bars to the suit for restitution of conjugal rights in the ecclesiastical courts.

15. What, or whether any thing besides adultery and cruelty, shall be deemed bars in the new court is not expressly stated in the statute ; section seventeen merely saying that the court

may decree restitution of conjugal rights, on being satisfied of the truth of the allegations, and that there is no legal ground why the decree should not be pronounced.

16. The court has a discretionary power. Suppose, therefore, a man guilty of an infamous offence; suppose him civilly dead; can he sue for restitution of conjugal rights? Suppose him actually in jail, or undergoing a sentence of transportation, will the court compel his wife to share his imprisonment, or accompany him to the penal settlement? Here neither the act of parliament nor the canon law furnishes a chart. The court, however, will be at no loss to decide the question when it arises.

17. The French law exacts a high reach of duty from the wife. Thus, where a married couple in Paris had a daughter dangerously ill of scarlet fever, the husband prohibited the wife from going to a ball. She, nevertheless, persisted in going, and went. On her return she found the door closed against her. The Tribunal of the Seine last spring pronounced in the husband's favour. In other words, they held that the wife could not sustain a suit for "restitution of conjugal rights;" for she was grossly in the wrong, not only as a wife, but as a mother.

18. Either party dissatisfied with any decision of the judge ordinary alone may, within three calendar months, appeal to the full court, whose decision shall be final; sect. 55.

19. But what if the decision has not been by the judge ordinary alone, but by the judge ordinary with one, or more, of the other judges of the said court?

CHAPTER XVII.

JACTITATION OF MARRIAGE.

1. SUITS for repressing jactitation (that is to say, boasting by A that he or she is married to B when the fact is not so) were of frequent occurrence prior to Lord Hardwicke's Act, when clandestine and consensual marriages prevailed; see supra, p. 2.

2. But for upwards of a century there have not been, we believe, more than three or four suits for jactitation in all.

3. How to jactitate, and what is jactitation, may be best learnt by referring to the Duchess of Kingston's case, 20, State Trials, 538; Lindo v. Belisario, 1 Hagg. 216; Goldsmid v. Bromer, ib. 324; and Hawke v. Corri, 2 Hagg. Con. 281. This last was in 1820, since which time it is understood that no one has been impeached for jactitating.

4. The suit with this singular title having gone almost wholly out of use, the Lord Chancellor's Bills of 1854, 1856, and 1857 contained clauses abolishing it entirely, because (among other good reasons) the questions which it was calculated to raise had been found capable of being more conveniently tried by a suit of nullity.

5. The Commons, however, struck out the Lord Chancellor's abolition clause. Jactitation suits, consequently, are retained.

6. They resemble the Scotch proceeding called by the plainer name of "putting to silence." In fact the Scotch phrase was in use with the jurists of Doctors' Commons. Thus, in Goldsmid v. Bromer, 1 Hagg. 324, the court at the request of the complainant "decreed a sentence of perpetual silence against the jactitator."

Enough of jactitations.

These suits are not likely to trouble the new Court. They are here mentioned only for conformity.

CHAPTER XVIII.

MODE OF TAKING EVIDENCE.

1. THE general rule prescribed by the Act is, that all witnesses shall be examined orally in open Court; sect. 46. This general rule, however, is liable to be modified by "such Rules and Regulations" as the Court may establish.

2. But, independently of "such Rules and Regulations," there is, in section 46, an over-riding proviso, declaring that "parties shall be at liberty to verify their respective cases by affidavit." This proviso no "Rules" or "Regulations" can touch. So that parties not emulous of publicity, may, to a certain extent, escape it, under this proviso.

3. The deponents, however, shall be subject to cross-examination and re-examination orally, in open Court.

4. But, if the parties and the Court itself are satisfied, the cause, however important and difficult, may be wholly disposed of upon affidavit.

5. The words in the proviso, "except as herein-before provided," refer to the petition for damages in respect of crim. con., which must go before a jury—see Chapter XIII.,— and to the petition for divorce where the parties, or either of them, insist on having the contested matters of fact tried by a jury.—See Chapter VI.

6. By the 16 & 17 Vict. c. 47. it is enacted, that in any suit or proceeding depending in any ecclesiastical court in England or Wales, the Court, if it shall think fit, may summon before it, and examine, or cause to be examined, witnesses by word of mouth, and, either before or after examination, by deposition or affidavit; and notes of such evidence shall be taken down by the judge or registrar, or by such other person or persons, and in such manner, as the judge of the Court shall direct.

7. In a late case, Dr. Lushington laid it down as a general rule, that the Court will always accede to an application to examine witnesses vivâ voce, and where such application is intended for the whole cause, the pleadings must be concluded before any of the witnesses are examined.—Campbell v. Campbell, Weekly Reporter, 2d May, 1857.

CHAPTER XIX.

WITNESSES ABROAD, OR UNABLE TO ATTEND.

1. WHEN a witness is "*out of*" the jurisdiction, the Court may order a commission to issue for the examination of such witness on interrogatories, or otherwise; sect. 47.

2. For this purpose all the powers given by the 13 Geo. 3. c. 63. and the 1 Will. 4. c. 22., enabling the Courts at Westminster to issue commissions, and to give directions respecting them, are extended to the Court "for Divorce and Matrimonial Causes."

3. The provisons of 13 Geo. 3. c. 63. are contained in sect. 44. thereof, which enacts that on any proceeding at law or in equity in any of the courts at Westminster, *for which cause has arisen in India,* the Court may award a commission to the Indian judges for the examination of witnesses, and the same, on being duly returned, shall be deemed competent evidence at any trial or hearing in such cause or action.

4. The 1 Will. 4. c. 22. s. 1. enacts, that the powers given by the 13 Geo. 3. c. 63. shall be extended to the Colonies, and to all actions depending in the courts of law at Westminster, wheresoever the cause of action may have arisen; wherever, in short, it shall appear that the issuing of a commission will be necessary, or conducive, to the due administration of justice.

5. The same statute of 1 Will. 4. c. 22., by its 4th section authorizes the issuing of a commission for the examination of witnesses at "any" place or places out of the jurisdiction, by interrogatories or otherwise; and the Court is empowered to give proper directions as to the manner and time of the

examination, and all other matters and circumstances connected therewith.

6. The affidavit in support of the application for a commission, the order granting the commission, the form of the commission, the interrogatories on both sides, the cross interrogatories, the time for the examination, the notice thereof, the return or report of the commission, are matters of detail.

7. The 10th section of the 1 Will. 4. c. 22. restricts (except by consent) the reading of depositions taken under the commission, until it be made to appear that the witnesses are really beyond the jurisdiction. The signature of the commissioner certifying the depositions need not be proved.

8. Where, again, a witness is *within* the jurisdiction, but where by reason of the illness of such witness, or from other circumstances, the Court shall not think fit to enforce the attendance of such witness in open court, it may order the examination of such witness on oath upon interrogatories, or otherwise, before any of its officers ; or before any other person to be named in the order for the purpose.

9. In this case also, as in the case of the commission, the provisions of 13 Geo. 3. c. 63. and 1 Will. 4. c. 22. are extended to the " Court for Divorce and Matrimonial Causes."

10. An affidavit will be necessary to obtain the order for such examination. The order to be made thereon, the interrogatories for the petitioner and respondent; the notice of the time for the examination ; and the order to be made, if necessary, for compelling the attendance of the witness before the examiner ; all these are matters of detail.

11. The 10th section of the 1 Will. 4. c. 22. restricts, except by consent, the reading of the depositions before such examiner until it be made to appear that the examinant is dead, or unable, from permanent sickness or other permanent infirmity, to attend in open court. The signature of the person taking the depositions need not be proved.

CHAPTER XX.

INTERVENTION OF JURIES.

1. WHEN questions of fact arise, a trial by jury may be directed, either before the Court itself or before any one or more of the judges thereof, and the jury may be either special or common; sect. 36. It is not obligatory on the Court to grant such trial except on petitions for damages in respect of crim. con.,—see Chapter XIII.,—and on petitions for divorce, where the parties, or either of them, insist on having the contested matters of fact tried by a jury; see Chapter VI.

2. The Court or judge may make all proper orders for the attendance of a special or common jury, and may give all other necessary directions; sect. 37.

3. The like qualifications in the jury, and the like rights of challenge in the parties, shall exist as at an ordinary trial before any of the superior courts; sect. 37.

4. The question for trial shall be in such form as the Court shall direct, and the judge shall have powers similar to those which belong to a judge at Nisi Prius; sect. 38.

5. Upon the trial a bill of exceptions may be tendered; and a general or special verdict or verdicts, subject to a special case, may be returned, as in a cause tried in any of the superior courts; sect. 39.

6. Where the trial shall not have been had in the "Court for Divorce and Matrimonial Causes," every such bill of exceptions, special verdict, and special case respectively, shall be returned into such court without any writ of error or other writ; sect. 39.

7. The matter of law arising on such bill of exceptions, special verdict, and special case, shall be determined by the

full Court, "subject to such right of appeal as is herein-after " given in other cases;" sect. 39.

8. The Court for Divorce and Matrimonial Causes may, as is done in Chancery, direct issues to be tried in any court of common law, either before a judge of assize, or at the sittings for the trial of causes in London or Westminster; sect. 40.

CHAPTER XXI.

JUDGE OF ASSIZE AND HIS NOMINEE.

1. JUDICIAL separation and restitution of conjugal rights may be applied for by petition to any judge of the assizes held for the county in which the husband and wife reside or last resided together ; sect. 17.

2. Such judge shall hear and determine such petition according to the rules and regulations which shall be made under the authority of the Act, sect. 17. Till those rules and regulations appear, he can do nothing.

3. On being satisfied of the truth of the allegations, and on being further satisfied that there is no legal ground why the prayer of the petition should not be granted, he may decree judicial separation or restitution of conjugal rights.

4. He may make provision for the custody, maintenance, and education of children.

5. When the application is by the wife, he may award alimony.

6. He may refer the petition to any of Her Majesty's counsel or serjeants-at-law named in the commission, and on the nomination of such counsel or serjeant, such counsel or serjeant shall, for the purpose of such nomination, have all the powers that the judge himself would have had, supposing him to have acted in his own person, and not by a nominee.

7. The orders in these matters shall be entered as orders of the Court, and shall be enforced as such.

8. Such orders shall be subject to the review of the judge ordinary ; but the appeal shall not stay execution unless the judge ordinary shall so order.

9. The Court shall from time to time regulate fees on these itinerant proceedings.

CHAPTER XXII.

ORDERS PROTECTING WIFE'S EARNINGS AND PROPERTY.

1. "A FRENCH washerwoman pestered by an idle drunken husband wipes the soap off her arms, leaves her work for half an hour, and returns with a certificate which protects her wages; an Englishwoman has no resource but to make terms with the vagabond. So long as he only robs her, and does not do her violence, the law holds him to be acting in his right."*

2. Lord St. Leonards, observing the excellent working of the French law (see the washerwoman's case, infra, p. 140), proposed clauses to give the English wife a privilege similar to that enjoyed by the French one. His lordship pressed the point in the Upper House with much vigour and perseverance. What opposition he encountered was overcome, not merely by the weight of reason, but by what is often more effective, the authority of a great legal name.

3. Lord St. Leonards' clauses (for there were two of them)

---

* Times, 18th March 1857.

applied solely to women thrown by the marital desertion on their own industry for support.

4. But the Commons made of the two clauses *one*, which now constitutes the twenty-first section of the act, and a very important section it is.

5. This section is not confined to women of the humbler or working class. It embraces high and low.

6. It seems immaterial whether the desertion commenced before or after the statute came into operation.

7. The wife's application may be made to a police magistrate when she is resident within the metropolitan district; to justices in petty sessions when she is resident in the country; and in every case whatever to the Court of Divorce.

8. The application may be ex parte. There is no provision for notice to the husband or to his creditors.

9. When the application is made to the Court of Divorce it will be heard by the Judge Ordinary. If he refuse, his decision may be submitted to the review of the "Full Court," within three months. Sect. 55.

10. When the application is made to a police magistrate, or to justices in petty sessions, and they refuse, the act gives no appeal.

11. The order will be an order protecting the wife's earnings and property acquired since the commencement of the desertion; and such earnings and property shall belong to her as if she were a feme sole; and she shall be in the like position with regard to property and conracts, and suing and be sued, as she would have been supposing her to have obtained a judicial separation.

12. What the position of a woman judicially separated will be, has been stated already, Chapter XI. It would seem that the order of protection will continue operative notwithstanding the renewal of cohabitation, so as that all such property as the wife may be entitled to when such cohabitation shall take place, shall be held to her separate use, as in the case of judicial separation, to which the case of a protecting order is expressly likened by section 21. The likeness, however, is not perfect, because a protecting order is

H

liable to be discharged, which a decree for judicial separation is not.

13. The requisite, that she " is maintaining herself by her " own industry or property," seems to preclude an application until some time after the commencement of the desertion ; because, supposing her to apply the instant her husband leaves her, she would not then be in a situation to show that she was "maintaining herself by her own industry or " property."

14. Every order of protection made by a police magistrate, or by justices, shall within ten days be entered with the Registrar of the County Court.

15. There may be some advantage, especially if the property is considerable, in applying to the Court of Divorce rather than to a magistrate or justices ; because, when the Court refuses the order, the refusal may be reviewed, and, when the Court grants the order, registration is unnecessary.

16. If the husband or any of his creditors shall seize or continue to hold property of the wife after notice of the protecting order, he shall be liable to a suit by the wife for the restoration of the specific property, and also for a sum equal to double its value.

17. Provision is made for the discharge of the protecting order by these words : "It shall be lawful for the husband, and " any creditor or other person claiming under him, to apply " to the court or to the magistrate or justices by whom such " order was made for the discharge thereof."

18. It perhaps would not have been improper to require that the woman making the application should be sworn. Every judge, however, has power to administer an oath, and he may say that without an oath he is not "satisfied" within the meaning of the act.

19. It appears that the metropolitan police magistrates have been already in several instances applied to for protecting orders. In one case, a solicitor for the wife stated, "that " about five weeks ago the husband returned, and, taking " from her forty shillings which she had earned, left her to " pay three quarters' rent and a number of bills; telling her " at the same time that she might go to the workhouse if she

" could not pay them." Upon this the magistrate observed,
" I don't think your application comes within the meaning
" of the Act of Parliament. The husband has only left her
" five weeks, and may return to-morrow." The application
was refused. The Act does not say how long the desertion is
to be. It must, however, be sufficiently long to put the woman
on her resources, whether of body or mind. This seems the
test. It may arise in less than " five weeks."

20. The injury under this section is not the desertion, but
the reappearance and the tyrannical use made of the marital
power. The wife seeks protection not because the husband
has gone away, but because he has come back and plundered
her, or may do both. This seems to be Lord St. Leonards'
view, for his lordship represents the mischief as consisting in
the fact of the husband "returning only to rob his wife of
her miserable earnings." * Who does not see that the very
best thing for the wife would be to make his desertion perpetual?

21. The French law does not require desertion, because the
protecting order may often be more useful when the husband
burdens his wife by a too constant adherence,—living at home
idly on her industry, or squandering in dissipation out of
doors her savings. Section 21 will probably be soon
amended.

22. In a case before the borough magistrates of Leeds, it
appeared that the husband had deserted his wife on the 13th
March 1848, and that she had since, by her own industry,
acquired property, consisting of eleven houses, furniture,
money, &c. The husband did not appear. The order was
very properly made at once.

23. It is not wonderful that magistrates should begin by
pronouncing some odd decisions; for the twenty-first section
would have puzzled Lord Mansfield himself. This case has
just occurred before the Mayor of Exeter:—The applicant for
a protecting order stated that her husband had not only
deserted her for five years, but had committed bigamy, for
which he was in prison awaiting his trial. She further stated
that in June last he came to her house utterly destitute; and
she, not knowing of the bigamy, gave him shelter, which,

* Handy Book, p. 76.

indeed, she was bound to do. As she was prospering in the occupation to which she had betaken herself, his creditors threatened to overwhelm her. The mayor refused the order, observing that the first desertion was got over by the husband's reappearance in June, and that the second desertion was but the involuntary consequence of incarceration! * As the rulings of the Court are to instruct the inferior magistrates, it is to be hoped that those rulings will not be in chambers.

24. A protecting order will operate retrospectively to the date of the desertion. A judicial separation only from the date of the sentence ; see supra, p. 63. It may be expedient, therefore, in many cases, to use both remedies.

25. In general it will be safer to make the protecting order than to refuse it, because it is always open to the husband or his creditors to have it discharged.

26. A prudent woman obtaining a protecting order will put the money, if the property consist of money, in the savings bank or some other security, in her own name ; because as to it she will be a feme sole. If she omit this precaution, her husband may lay his hands on her savings whenever he thinks proper to present himself, for she cannot shut her door against him. And this shows the difference between the position of a wife armed with a protecting order and that of a wife judicially separated.

27. It appears probable that protecting orders will in many cases render judicial separation unnecessary. They will improve the qualities of husbands, by showing them that they are not to have everything their own way.

---

* Times, 29th January 1858.

CHAPTER XXIII.

PROTEST AGAINST THE DEFECTS OF THE DIVORCE BILL; SIGNED BY LORD LYNDHURST.

On the 23rd June, 1857, the Divorce and Matrimonial Causes Bill having been read the third time in the House of Lords, an amendment was moved to strike out the word " *incestuous* " contained in the clause allowing divorce to the wife where her husband was guilty of incestuous adultery; see section 27 of the Act, and Chapter V., supra, p. 31. The proposed amendment, however, was rejected, though supported by Lord Lyndhurst. Against this vote of rejection the following powerful expression of dissent is entered in the Journals, and is here inserted as a guide for further legislation :—

1. Because the effect of rejecting this amendment will be to confine the dissolution of marriage upon the adultery of the husband to the four cases* stated in the bill, which we consider to be not only inexpedient, but, as contrasted with the relief upon the adultery of the wife, partial and unjust.

2. Because, as the clause is framed, although the husband should be living in the most open and notorious adultery, and should even bring his mistress into the family residence,†

---

* See Chapter 5 supra, p. 30. The number of cases, in the *Act*, is more than " four." The Commons expanded the remedy.

† At the instigation of Lord John Manners, and with the concurence of Lord John Russell, the Commons inserted a clause giving the wife divorce when her husband " committed adultery in the conjugal residence;" a most reasonable and excellent clause, and a great improvement on the corresponding one in the Code Napoleon, though the objects of both are evidently the same, namely, to secure domestic purity, and save the wife from an " odious rivalry." The truth is,

insulting the wife by her presence, and should endeavour by ill-usage to compel her to submit to this disgrace, such a case would not come within its provisions.

3. Because the adultery of the husband, accompanied with the commission of the greatest crimes, and even the most infamous vices, would not entitle the wife to relief under this clause.

4. Because the adultery of the husband, although coupled with his condemnation to penal servitude, even for life, and the consequent degradation and misery of the wife, would not, under the provisions of this bill, enable her to obtain a dissolution of her marriage.

.5. Because many other cases of similar injustice and hardship are excluded from relief under this clause.

6. Because to allow a divorce for the adultery of the wife, and to refuse it in these and other cases of adultery by the husband, coupled with acts of deep injury inflicted upon the wife, is manifestly unjust.

7. Because, although the adultery of the wife may lead to the imposing a spurious offspring on the husband, and entitle him to a divorce for a reason which would not apply to the case of adultery by the husband, other circumstances may and frequently do occur in connection with the adultery of the husband, giving the wife an equal claim to this remedy.

---

legislation will continue unsatisfactory till the views of Lord Lyndhurst in the one House, and Mr. Gladstone in the other, are made good. I say Mr. Gladstone, because, although originally opposed to divorce, he declared at the outset that if divorce were to be granted at all, it must be on the principle of equal justice to both the sexes. To the vindication of this principle he directed all his powers of reasoning and argument, assisted, not impeded, by the indignant fervour of scornful eloquence. Here, too, the Attorney-General gave in readily, in spite of the duty cast upon him; and he denounced the refusal of all redress to the wife as " opprobrious and wicked." Mr. Gladstone said, " the admission of the Attorney-General does him honour." By the principle of equal justice, however, we do not mean that a single act of adultery by the husband is as bad as a single act of adultery by the wife. When she commits adultery the husband's remedy ought to be peremptory; when he is guilty the Court should have a discretion. To make justice equal we must measure the injury. See what is said as to the plea of recrimination, supra, Chapter VII., p. 43.

Lord John Manners' clause, however, was struck out on the return of the Bill to the Lords, notwithstanding the support of Lord Cranworth and the rest of the Government.

8. Because no distinction is made in Scripture between the case of the man and of the woman in the commission of adultery. The sin is the same in both—both are included under the same prohibition.

9. Because the whole tendency and spirit of the Christian religion is manifestly calculated to raise women to equal rights and equal responsibilities with men. "It has," in the words of an eminent writer on general law (Chief Justice Story), " elevated woman to the rank and dignity of an equal, instead " of being an humble companion or a devoted slave of her hus- " band;" and accordingly we find that as Christianity extended itself, and its influence was brought to bear upon social and civil affairs, so the condition of woman was improved, and her rights to protection and redress were acknowledged. With respect to marriage and divorce, the rule of the Roman Catholic church applies to both sexes equally, while all Protestant legislatures (except our own), in declaring that marriage may be dissolved for the cause of adultery, have accorded to the wife the same rights and remedies as to the husband.

10. Because by our Ecclesiastical Law (the only law at present applicable to this subject) the same judgment is pronounced in the case of adultery, whether the crime be committed by the husband or the wife; and there appears to us no reason why, in extending the remedy, the principle should be changed.

11. Because as to the objection that the extension of the law to cases of adultery by the husband will give occasion to a great number of suits for divorce, we think such apprehension is altogether groundless. The proceedings can originate only with the wife, and she has, both as to feeling and interest, so much at stake, so much to relinquish which must be most dear to her, that we think there is little fear of her resorting to this remedy except in extreme cases, and after all hope of amendment has ceased.

12. Because by the law of Scotland the adultery of the husband with respect to divorce is placed on the same footing with the adultery of the wife. This law is found to be attended with no inconvenience. The evidence upon the subject is above all exception, and we deem it most desirable

that laws which so deeply affect the social and moral condition of the people should, in contiguous parts of the same empire, be in accordance with each other.

HUTCHINSON.
HARRINGTON.
LYNDHURST.
TALBOT DE MALAHIDE.
BELMORE.

CHAPTER XXIV.

THAT FIVE YEARS' DESERTION SHOULD BE A GROUND FOR DIVORCE; BY LORD LYNDHURST.

On the 23rd June, 1857, Lord Lyndhurst moved the insertion of a clause which would have entitled the wife to divorce where her husband had been " guilty of wilful desertion without reasonable cause for five years or upwards." This having been objected to, the question was put, and Lord Lyndhurst's motion was negatived. Against this vote Lord Lyndurst's protest is entered in the Journals. The following are the grounds on which his Lordship rested his dissent, namely:—

1. Because the contract of marriage is the most solemn engagement into which a man can enter, and in which he promises to love, comfort, and honour the woman, and keep her under all circumstances of sickness or of health, and adhere to her as long as they shall both live.

2. Because the purposes of this engagement, as deduced from Scripture, are of the deepest interest and importance— viz., for the birth of children to be brought up in the love and fear of God, for a remedy against sin, and for mutual society, help, and comfort, both in prosperity and adversity.

3. Because by wilful desertion not only is this sacred promise impiously violated, but all the purposes for which this ordinance of God was instituted are wholly frustrated. Even in the most ordinary contract the breach of it on the one side puts an end to the obligation on the other, and we see no reason why a different rule should be applied to the contract of marriage, and more especially in a case destructive of the entire objects of the union. It appears to us to be contrary to all principle, and most unjust, that the husband should be permitted to set at naught an engagement followed, as it must

be, by such consequences, and that the woman should continue to be bound by it.

4. Because we feel strongly the extreme cruelty of such conduct towards the deserted wife, in the utter disappointment of all her confident expectations of happiness from the promised love, comfort, and society of her husband, and leaving her without hope to the contemplation of a long, dreary, and desolate future.

5. Because divorce from this cause is justified as scriptural by the highest ecclesiastical authorities. It is well known that at the Reformation the subject was anxiously and carefully considered by prelates and divines eminent for learning and piety, and that they came to the conclusion that wilful desertion was a scriptural ground for divorce. We find the names of Archbishop Cranmer, of the Bishops of London, of Winchester, Ely, Exeter, and others, of Latimer, Parker, &c., of Peter Martyr, Martin Bucer, Beza, Luther, Melancthon, Calvin, &c., among those who maintained this opinion, and which was adopted by the whole body of Protestants on the continent of Europe. Accordingly, this has been the acknowledged doctrine of all their churches to the present day. We find the same doctrine expressly stated and adopted in the eighth article on divorce in the Reformatio Legum Ecclesiasticarum, compiled under the authority of Henry the Eighth and Edward the Sixth, which body of laws, although it did not receive the confirmation of the Crown, in consequence of the early and unexpected death of King Edward, has always, as the Commissioners on the Law of Divorce, in their Report, justly observe, been considered of great authority. We also find that at a more recent period a right reverend prelate, eminent for learning and talents (Cozens, Bishop of Durham), in his celebrated argument delivered in this house in the case of Lord Roos, maintained the same opinion. His words are these:—" The promise of constancy in the marriage ceremony " does not extend to tolerating adultery or malicious deser- " tion, *which dissolve the marriage.*"

6. Because, by the law of Scotland, wilful desertion, as in all the Protestant churches on the continent, is considered to be a scriptural ground for divorce, and the law in this respect is regarded by all the first authorities in that country, not

only to be free from inconvenience, but as just and highly beneficial. We further deem it to be most desirable that upon such a subject as marriage and divorce, affecting as it does the whole social system, the same law should, as far as practicable, prevail in both parts of the kingdom, and the more so as continued experience has shown the great inconvenience occasioned by the difference and anomalies of the two systems.

7. Because, as to the objections to the proposed extension of this measure on the ground of its tendency to demoralize society, this is not only disproved by the example of Scotland, but a careful examination of the state of society in Roman Catholic countries will, we think, lead to the conclusion that the principle of the indissolubility of marriage is far less favourable to morality than the opposite doctrine, accompanied with a cautious exercise of the power of divorce in such extreme cases as those of adultery and malicious desertion.

8. Because, as to what is urged with reference to the law of our Ecclesiastical Courts, we answer that the object of the present bill throughout is to amend that law, and to render it more consistent with reason and justice; and with respect to the Church of England, we will merely repeat what we find stated in the argument of the learned prelate to which we have already referred, viz., that "we cannot see why *they* are " to be styled the Church of England who join with the " Council of Trent rather than *those* who join with all the " reformed churches, and plead against the canon of the Church " of Rome, which hath laid an anathema upon us if we do " not agree with them."

LYNDHURST.
HUTCHINSON.

CHAPTER XXV.

AUTHORITIES AND ILLUSTRATIONS.

1. CRUELTY.

Mr. N—— left his wife Lady C—— N. at Coulson's hotel in the sitting room with the door locked; and on the same evening, after two hours' absence, he returned, and she, hearing his arrival, withdrew into the bed-room and bolted the door, which he endeavoured, but without effect, to break open; soon after Lady C——— came into the sitting room, which was open, and one of the waiters took hold of her and pushed her back, and on her telling him he had no business to touch her, he replied that he did so by order of Mr. N——; Mr. N—— then came to the door and dragged his wife back to the sitting room with great force and violence, saying "she might take herself off the next day where she pleased, but she " should not go out that night." (She wished to go to her father's.) At 7 o'clock the same evening Lady H——C., sister of Lady C——, came to Coulson's hotel; on Lady C—— accompanying her said sister to the door, Mr. N—— again caught hold of her and pulled her back with such force and violence as occasioned her great pain, and the marks and bruises occasioned thereby were seen by many persons, and were visible for several days. Per Dr. Lushington: "Assuming that all this was with- " out excuse, there still appears nothing to induce me to arrive at the " conclusion that Lady C—— cannot return to cohabition without the " risk of personal violence."—N—— v. N——, 4. Hagg, Ecc. Rep.

Per Lord Brougham: "That the ground of the remedy is confined to " personal violence is not my opinion of the law of England, and I am " quite clear as to the law of Scotland. I am convinced that the law is " nearly, if not altogether, the same in the two countries. It is not true " that the law of England requires either actual injury to the person, or " threat of such injury."—Paterson v. Russell, 7 Bell, App. Ca. 337.

There may be a systematic persecution without blows; thus, per Lord Brougham: "Suppose a man were continually charging his wife with every " sort of immoral and criminal conduct, and there was not the shadow of " a foundation for those charges made before her family, her friends, rela- " tions, and servants, and in the face of the world, I have little doubt that " what now rests only upon opinions would ultimately assume the form of " decision, namely, that to such injurious treatment, making the marriage " state impossible to be endured, and rendering life itself almost unbearable, " the probabilty is very high that the Consistory Courts of this country

" would extend the remedy of divorce à mensâ et thoro."—Paterson v. Russell, 7 Bell, App. Ca. 337.

In a Scotch case, nearly a century ago, the allegation against the husband was, that he " Disliked and shunned his wife, ceased to cohabit with her, " refused to salute her, took away her child from her, and sent her victuals " by a common street porter." These facts being proved, the court awarded to her separate alimony; and the decision, under the advice of Lord Chancellor Camden and Lord Mansfield, was affirmed by the House of Lords.— Arthur v. Gourlay, 2 Paton's Rep. 184.

It has been said that "The court has no gauge for the diversities of " rank and fortune in estimating cruelty;" but this seems wrong. Says Dr. Lushington: " The means and rank of the parties must raise some " distinctions. Necessaries and comforts must always bear some relation to the " rank and station of the parties. Where they are in totally different ranks of " life, the words ' necessaries and comforts' have different significations. A " wife brought up as a gentlewoman would suffer in her health and con- " stitution, nay, her life might be endangered by a mode of living which " would be even comfortable to a female of a different grade."
It is remarkable that although Dr. Lushington expressed these sentiments in the Countess of D——'s case, he nevertheless refused her redress. His sentence, however, was reversed by Sir Herbert Jenner Fust, who held that Lady D—— could not be called upon to return to her husband. Yet in the way of personal violence, the strongest thing charged against Lord D—— was but a forcible holding of her hands, and his saying that he would "thrash her if the law allowed him." Sir H. J. Fust, however, said " when I see that the husband has recourse to any sort of treatment short " of ' thrashing' his wife, I cannot say that the Countess can with safety " return to her husband." In course of his judgment Sir Herbert refers to the acquired feelings and tastes incident to high rank—the delicacy of a wife brought up so tenderly—herself of noble birth—her consequent unfitness to sustain such usage—withal the husband's great fortune—his squalid estab- lishment—dilapidated house—faded furniture—and coarse fare,—even the hard salt beef and the solitary eight dip candle are adverted to. All these enumerated particulars dwelt upon by the judge in determining the point of cruelty show that the court *has* a " gauge," and makes use of it on proper occasions.—D—— v. D——, 1 Rob. 106, 3 Ecc. Notes, 340. The French jurists are still more attentive to the like considerations.—See the remarks of M. Demolombe respecting Separations, *infra*, p. 136.

Threat by a husband " to throw a knife in his wife's face," coupled with another fact, namely, that he "thrust his fist in her mouth, she having a " child in her arms." Separation pronounced.—Harris v. Harris, 2 Hagg. Con. 148.

Spitting in the face is an old ground of divorce à mensâ et thoro.— Cloburn's case, Hetley, 149. It is justified by Dr. Lushington as being a gross personal insult.—5 Notes of Cases, 418. It is an act of cruelty, though certainly not injurious to life or limb. The delicate constitution of the wife aggravated the cruelty. She was treated with indignity and severity. The husband called her by opprobrious names, swore at her, &c.—Otway v. Otway, 2 Phill. 98.

The communication of an infamous disease is a strong ground for judicial separation.—Collett *v.* Collett, 1 Curt. 678. Ciocci *v.* Ciocci, 1 Spinks. 21.

Per Sir John Nicholl: " I cannot conceive cruelty of a more grievous " character (except perhaps great personal violence) than the accusation— " incest—made by this gentleman against his wife."—Bray *v.* Bray, 1 Hagg. Ecc. 167. See M. Demolombe to the same effect, infra, p. 136, and Lord Brougham, supra, p. 108.

Per Sir W. Scott: The wife may have, by provocation, brought on herself " the ill-treatment complained of. When that appears, she is not entitled to " demand relief."—Waring *v.* Waring, 2 Hagg. Con. 153.

For cruelty inflicted by the wife on her husband, divorce à mensâ et thoro pronounced by Sir W. Scott.—Kirkman *v.* Kirkman, 1 Hagg. Con. 409.

To a suit for judicial separation in respect of adultery, cruelty was not in the Ecclesiastical Courts an available defence, for which a reason was given more technical than solid; namely, that compensation could arise only where the parties were in eodem delicto. But, per Dr. Lushington: " I entertain " great doubts whether the reason is satisfactory." Well might this eminent judge say so, for under the rule a man was allowed to demand divorce à mensâ et thoro against his wife for adultery, although he had by his cruelty driven her to the act. The Divorce Report disapproves of all this, p. 17; and, what is more material, the Statute, by its thirty-first section, seems to forbid it.

---

2. DESERTION.

The court in process of time will define desertion. As it is a new head of jurisdiction, there are no cases and no authorities, for the Ecclesiastical Courts took no cognizance of it, and this, apparently, because Sanchez, their oracle, ignored it.

Dr. Johnson defines desertion to be "the act of forsaking or abandoning."

The Scotch cases do not furnish a test of desertion. It appears to be considered that the offence may take place, although the parties reside in the same locality. It is not necessary that the deserting party should leave the country. The duty broken is the duty of nuptial cohabitation. If this should be ruled to be the law of England under the new Act, the following question, put by Mr. Henley in debate can have but one answer:—" Suppose a man of fortune to have a house in Eaton Square, " where he maintained his wife with a liberal establishment, an equipage " suitable to her rank, and everything furnished at her husband's expense. " But then suppose him to reside apart from his wife in a different region of " the metropolis. Would this be desertion?" If we anticipate an affirmative decision, it will follow that the mere supplying of necessaries, or even the allowance of superfluities to a wife, would be no answer to her complaint against a husband who repudiated her society.

The foreign codes do not throw much light on this matter.

" A simple absence," according to Lord Stair, "will not constitute wilful " desertion." There must be, says Erskine, " a deliberate purpose of " abandoning the conjugal society."

Per Lord Cockburn : " These decrees are not made merely for default of " appearance, but on such evidence as shall satisfy the court of the fact of " desertion."—Anderson v. Anderson, 2d Series of Scotch Decisions, vol. iv. p. 616.

It is remarkable that the Code Napoléon is silent as to desertion. This is the more curious, because the French law of the 20th September 1792 dealt not only with cases of desertion, but with cases of mere absence without intelligence. Thus, Art. 5 allows divorce "sur l'abandon de la femme " par le mari, ou du mari par la femme, pendant deux ans au moins." Art. 6 allows divorce " sur l'absence de l'un d'eux sans nouvelles au moins " pendant cinq ans."

The Scotch summons sets forth the marriage, and the time, place, and manner of the desertion.—1 Shand's Scotch Prac. 436.

Where the defendant is out of the jurisdiction, the citation to found a sentence of divorce for desertion may be edictal.—1 Shand's Scotch Prac. 437.

Where the deserter had returned and offered to renew cohabitation just when the sentence of divorce was about to be pronounced—
Per Lord Mackenzie : " If a tender of adherence can still be received from " this defender to the effect of rendering abortive the pursuer's whole " previous proceedings, the same steps may again and again be repeated."
Per Lord Corehouse : " The remedy was meant to be effectual. The " party deserted has a right to obtain a divorce, a jus quæsitum not to be " defeated at the option of the deserter by a subsequent tender of adhe- " rence."—Murray v. Maclachlan, Scotch Cases, 21st Dec. 1838.

Per Professor More : " There is scarcely any part of our Scotch law which " is in a more unsatisfactory state than our doctrine of desertion. No " proper definition has been given of desertion further than that it must be " wilful and malicious."

Per Professor More : " I observe, in the recent statute (Sections 27 " and 31), that the adultery of the husband, coupled with desertion *without* " *reasonable excuse* for two years, will entitle a wife to apply for divorce. The " great point, therefore, in the construction of this statute, will be to ascer- " tain what will be held a ' *reasonable excuse.*' "

In Morgan v. Morgan it appeared that the marriage had taken place on the 24th April, 1837, the husband being at the time not quite seventeen, and the wife but eighteen or nineteen. The husband, who was then at school, had considerable expectations from his father and grandfather. The wife was shewn to have been virtuous before the marriage, and chaste after it for two years and a half.   But then it came out that a very few days after the marriage the husband had been sent to the continent, and subsequently to India. That the smallest consideration was paid to the wife's protection or maintenence there was no proof whatever. Upon this state of circumstances the learned judge, Dr. Lushington, observed : " She, a girl of nineteen, of " great personal beauty, recently married, is at once left—I will not say to " the risk, but almost to the certainty, of destruction. That such an example " can be otherwise than prejudicial to public morals cannot for a moment be " stated. But I find, from my own notes, that in Reeves v. Reeves (2 Phil. " 125), Sir John Nicholl declared that the wilful desertion of a wife was no " bar to a suit against her for adultery; and in Sullivan v. Sullivan " (2 Add. 302) the same doctrine is repeated. I am bound to administer " the law as I find it. I pronounce for the divorce." Dr. Lushington, on a subsequent occasion (Dillon v. Dillon, 3 Curt. 91), alluding to this decision, acknowledges that he had some " doubts as to the propriety of this " doctrine, although compelled to act upon it in Morgan v. Morgan."— 2 Curteis, 688.

The above cases can hardly be law now, because desertion is one of the discretionary bars to divorce under Section 31 (see supra, p.   ); and it will probably be held to be no less a bar to judicial separation. Dr. Lushington owns that desertion, no less than cruelty, has " a tendency to cause the wife " to commit adultery."—Dillon v. Dillon, 3 Curt. 91.   The Commissioners in their report, p. 17, hold that desertion should be a bar to a suit "for " separation or divorce on what ground soever the relief may be sought."

3. LENOCINIUM.—THE HAVING BEEN ACCESSORY TO THE ADULTERY.—PROSTITUTION.

Lord Audley was accused and convicted of " holding his wife by force while " one of his minions forcibly, against her will, had carnal knowledge of " her. So that he was charged as præsens auxilians and comfortans, and " therefore a principal."—State Trials, 7 Cha. 1., 1631.

The common case in the police reports of a man sending his wife to the streets to get money by prostitution.

Per Sir W. Scott: " If the husband contrives the meeting, the offence is " prostitution, and more than connivance."—Timmings v. Timmings, 3 Hagg. Ecc. Rep. 78.

Per Sir W. Scott, speaking of connivance : " The expression in the books " of a man prostituting his wife, 'Vir qui uxorem prostituit,' is too strong." —Moorson v. Moorson, 2. Hagg. Ecc. 107.

Lenocinium is a bar to divorce when sought for by the husband. It comprehends all that misconduct by which the husband becomes the pander to his wife's guilt, exposes her to pollution, or encourages and promotes licentious conduct.—Sir Geo. Mackenzie's Criminal Law : Head Adultery.

In one case lenocinium was argued to be only where the husband exposed his wife *for gain*. But it was successfully answered,—" The husband who " vitiates the mind of his wife ought to be repelled. The practices alleged " could be for no other purpose than by familiarizing her mind with lewdness, " to dispose her to actual adultery, and therefore ought to be regarded as " lenociny."—Mackenzie *v.* Mackenzie. Morrison's Dictionary of Scotch Decisions: Head *Adultery*.

Cibber's case, 1738. Cibber brought an action against a man for debauching his wife. It appeared that the plaintiff and defendant lived in the same house. Their bedrooms communicated. Mrs. Cibber used to undress in her husband's room, and retire to the defendant's, with a pillow taken from the bed of her husband, who shut the door after her and wished her good night. He sometimes called the defendant and Mrs. Cibber up to breakfast.—3 Hagg. Ecc. 120., and Selwyn's N. P. 10. This was Theophilus Cibber, son of the more reputable Colley. Theophilus is represented as " having entrapped his amiable wife into an illicit intercourse with a man " of fortune with a view to damages; but he got only 10*l.* and universal " execration; while, on the other hand, Mrs. Cibber, being regarded as the " victim of her dissolute husband, obtained both countenance and respect." So says the " Sequel to the Life of Colley Cibber," which, we presume, was written by a gentleman indulgently inclined to the female sex; for if it be true that Mrs. Cibber carried the pillow nightly from her husband's bed to that of her paramour, her delicacy may be questioned. But how came the jury to award even 10*l.* to the scamp Theophilus, who, it appears, was as unfortunate as he was profligate?

4. CONNIVANCE.

We are told by the very learned Dr. Lushington that the ecclesiastical doctrines as to connivance " are not what they ought to be."—Phillips *v.* Phillips, 1 Rob. Ecc. Rep. 156.

Per Dr. Lushington: " Of most culpable negligence, of the most supine " inattention, when his honour loudly called for the most active interposition, " I must say Mr. Phillips is guilty, but I acquit him of corrupt connivance. " In pronouncing for a separation I feel that I shall tolerate a negligent in- " attention to marital duty, and that I shall pronounce a decree which will " not lead to the peace and honour of families, nor to the purity of private " life. If such consequences of the law did not deter Lord Stowell, much " less should they deter me; foreseeing as he did, and lamenting as I do in " common with him, the effects they may have in matrimonial life."— Phillips *v.* Phillips, 1 Rob. Ecc. Rep. 144.

Per Sir W. Scott: " The husband is perfectly at liberty to let the " licentiousness of his wife take its full scope."—Timmings *v.* Timmings, 3 Hagg. Ecc. 78. This must be wrong. To connive (from conniveo), is to wink at a thing, which he certainly does who takes no notice of his wife's irregularities, but gives them " full scope."

Per Sir John Nicholl: "Active corruption is not necessary to constitute " connivance. Passive acquiescence with the intention and in the expectation " that guilt will follow is sufficient. There must be consent."—Rogers *v.* Rogers, 3 Hagg. Ecc. 57.

Major Gardener told his wife that he "wished she would do something to " put an end to the connection." Mrs. Gardener's riding and walking with the coachman had been notorious in the neighbourhood for a month before she quitted her husband, yet the bill passed.—Lords' Journ., Session 1837.

It appeared that Mr. Calcraft was perfectly aware of Mrs. Calcraft's intercourse with Lord Harborough. Bill to be read a second time that day six months.—Macq. H. of L., 656.

The wife may connive. It was pleaded that the wife was cognisant of the adultery, and acquiesced in it; that is, winked at it, which is the very definition of connivance. — Lady Kirkwall *v.* Lord Kirkwall, 2 Hagg. Con. 277.

.Connivance is deemed not inconsistent with a denial of guilt. Thus, per Sir W. Scott, the wife may say, "I deny criminality; and these appearances "into which I have been betrayed were the contrivance of my husband; " but I have not accomplished his intention."—Lovering *v.* Lovering, 3 Hagg. Ecc. 91.

Connivance is not constituted by mere disgusting and obscene language.— Cocksedge *v.* Cocksedge, 1 Rob. Ecc. 99.

Per Sir W. Scott: "The act of permitting his apprentice to remain an " inmate of his house after he knew of these indecent familiarities, is a delin- " quency which renders him unworthy of relief."—Timmings *v.* Timmings, 3 Hagg. Ecc. 84.

---

5. COLLUSION.

The Solicitor General *Wedderburn*, in the Duchess of Kingston's case, said, "A sentence obtained by collusion is no sentence. A sentence is a " judicial determination of a cause agitated between real parties, upon a real " interest, a real argument, a real prosecution, a real defence, a real decision. " Of all these requisites not one takes place in the case of a fraudulent and " collusive suit; there is no judge, but a person invested with the ensigns " of a judicial office is misemployed in listening to a fictitious cause pro- " posed to him; and, to use the words of a very sensible civilian, 'fabula " 'non judicium, hoc est; in scenâ, non in foro, res agitur.' "—20 State Tr. 355. The above has been quoted more than once with assent, if not with admiration, by Lord Chancellor Cranworth.

Where it came out that there had been a collusive contract respecting the verdict, the bill of divorce was abandoned.—Mrs. George's case, Macq. H. of L. 661.

. Where circumstances had been collusively suppressed at the trial, the bill of divorce was rejected.—Mr. Cope's case, Macq. H. of L. 593.

Where it appeared that the costs had been defrayed, not by the petitioning husband, but by the paramour, the bill of divorce was rejected.—Mr. Downe's case, Macq. H. of L. 584.

The husband was examined as to whether he had had any communication with the paramour since the wife's elopement. This was under an impression that the proceeding was collusive,—that is to say, by arrangement between the husband and the paramour.—Mr. Wilson's case, Lords' Journals, 26th April, 1798.

Where the costs had been defrayed, not by the petitioning husband, but by the father of the guilty wife, and where witnesses were produced against her, but none on her behalf,—the indications of collusion were such that the bill of divorce was rejected.—Mr. Chisim's case, Macq. H. of L. 583.

Per Sir W. Scott: "It is not collusion that after the adultery both parties. "are desirous to obtain a divorce."—Crewe v. Crewe, 3 Hagg. Ecc. 130.

Per Lord President Hope: "A summons of divorce, on the head of "adultery, must be looked on with a jealous eye when undefended."— Orde v. Orde, 8 Shaw's Scotch Rep. 50.

Collusion is an agreement between the parties for one to commit adultery, so that the other may obtain a remedy as for a real injury.—Crewe v. Crewe,. 3 Hagg. 130. The essence of collusion is the fraud on the court.

An Englishman and an Englishwoman intermarried in England. In March 1831, having no doubt heard of Scotch facilities, this couple repaired to Edinburgh, where they took no house, but hired apartments. After a forty days' residence, which constitutes a domicile, or founds a forum, under the Scotch law, the wife commenced a suit against her husband before the Court of Session for divorce, on the ground that during his short stay in Scotland he had been guilty of adultery. She made the usual oath that there was no collusion between herself and her husband. Towards the end of July, in the same year, both parties returned to England, leaving the suit to proceed under the care of the Scotch jurisdiction. Per the Lord Justice Clerk Boyle: "The question of collusion is not before us."—Goldney v. Goldney, 12 Court of Session Cases, 468. The facts suggested collusion, and the very remark of the learned judge showed that the question of collusion was "before him."

The joint expedition to Scotland, the seasonable adultery committed there, the accomplishment of the design which the parties may be supposed to have had in view, and their contemporaneous return to England, in full assurance that the divorce would be granted,—an assurance which, it would seem, was afterwards realised,—make this short case deserving the attention of the new court, and may serve to shew the value of the affidavit required by the 41st section of the 20 & 21 Vict. c. 85. See also Remarks on this topic suprà, p. 40.

Per Sir John Nicholl : " The court was jealous lest it might be made a " party to a scheme for getting a divorce more easily by a journey to Scotland." —Dunn *v.* Dunn, 2 Phill. 403.

A wife having brought an action for divorce on the ground of adultery against her husband, it was opposed by the trustee for his creditors as far as related to pecuniary consequences ; but the wife, upon oath, negatived collusion, and although the trustee offered a proof of collusion, yet the guilt of the husband was established. Held, 1, that the proof offered by the trustee after the oath was incompetent ; and, 2, that the wife was entitled to a decree of divorce without any qualification as to the right of the creditors.—Greenhill *v.* Aitken, 2 Shaw's Scotch Rep. 435. · It would seem that the oath excludes inquiry. If so, nothing can be worse than the Scotch practice on this head.

---

6. CONDONATION.

Knowledge of what is condoned must be distinctly proved.—Durant *v.* Durant, 1 Hagg. Ecc. 733.

In order to found a relevant defence of remissio injuriæ, it must be proved that the injured party was in the certain knowledge of particular acts of adultery, such as could found a divorce, but nevertheless cohabited thereafter with the guilty party.—Legrand *v.* Legrand, 2 Craigie and St., Scotch Rep. 596.

The plea of remissio injuriæ was sustained by the Court of Session ; but in the House of Lords the case was remitted for reconsideration, with considerable doubts expressed as to the judgment below, in consequence of there being no evidence that the husband had probable knowledge of his wife's guilt at the time of the alleged condonation.—Fairlie *v.* Fairlie, 6 Paton's Reports, 121.

Wife guilty of adultery, husband guilty too, but his guilt condoned by the wife. Divorce à mensâ et thoro pronounced against her.—Anichini *v.* Anichini, 2 Curt. 210.

Lord Stowell held it necessary for the husband to prove that he had not slept with his wife after his knowledge of her adultery.—Timmings *v.* Timmings, 3 Hagg. Ecc. 84.

The husband allowed his wife to remain three weeks in his house after the ascertainment of her adultery ; and it was proved that they dined together three times after the disclosure. Bill abandoned.—Mr. Miller's case, Macq. H. of L. 628.

Per Sir W. Scott : " Mere residence in the same house, without actual " conjugal cohabitation, will not amount to condonation. 'Si enim " ' essent in eadem domo, non se alloquentes, non censeretur condonatum " ' adulterium ' (Sanchez)."—1 Hagg. Ecc. 736.

Per Dr. Lushington: " I have always understood, that when a husband " has received reliable information as to his wife's guilt, although he is not " bound to remove her out of the house, he ought to cease marital cohabi- " tation with her. If he acts as if he credited the information, and yet con- " tinues to cohabit, he forfeits his right to reparation."—Dillon v. Dillon, 3 Curt. 91.

Per Sir W. Scott: " The fact of condonation is justly held less stringent " in the wife. It is a merit in her to bear, and endeavour to reclaim. It is " not her duty, till compelled by the last necessity, to have recourse to legal " remedies."—D'Aguilar v. D'Aguilar, 1 Hagg. Ecc. 786.

Per Lord Meadowbank: " The law will make great allowance for the " situation in which the wife is placed; without the means of leaving her " husband; generally of habits of indecision; in most instances unwilling " to drive matters to an extremity; in all, where there is a family, having " before her eyes the prospect of a separation from her children, and of " leaving them under the guardianship of one from whom they are not likely " to derive much attention or beneficial instruction. These considerations " must be allowed weight in all such cases; and, therefore, many circum- " stances will, where reconciliation is pleaded against a suit of divorce by " the wife, be often disallowed, although an opposite conclusion would be " deduced supposing the husband the complainant, because he is degraded " by exercising a forbearance which, on the wife's part, is often the result " of the most amiable feelings, and which, instead of lowering, not unfre- " quently exalts her character in the world."—Greenhill v. Ford, 2 Shaw's Scotch App. Ca. 442.

Divorce granted to the wife for cruelty, the alleged condonation having been under the influence of fear.—Turner v. Turner, 2 Spinks, 201.

Returning to the husband's bed held, under the circumstances, not a condonation of the previous cruelty.—Hart v. Hart, 2 Spinks, 193.

Per Sir W. Scott: " The husband's facility to condone shows that he does " not duly estimate the injury, and will make the court watch jealously his " subsequent conduct."—Timmings v. Timmings, 3 Hagg. Ecc. 78.

Per Lord Chancellor Brougham: " Mere surmises of condonation could not " deprive the petitioner of his remedy."—Colonel Clayton's case, Macq. H. of L. 661.

The petitioner's counsel were asked whether they could get over the difficulty of their own case, Mr. Perry having offered his wife 200l. a year if she would give up her adulterous connexion, she remaining his wife; an error into which he appeared to have fallen from the excess of kind feeling and the want of caution. Bill of divorce to be read a second time that day six months.—Mr. Perry's case, Macq. H. of L. 663. The decision took the late able and amiable Mr. Talbot (who was counsel for the petitioner) by surprise, for it did not appear that what Mr. Perry did was wrong. If the Bill had passed, it would have been accompanied by a bond binding him to do the thing for the doing of which it was rejected; nay, a worse thing,

for the "lady's friend" imposed no stipulation as to chastity. See supra,
p. 56.

Where the husband and wife ultimately parted on account of her being
great with the child begotten by the paramour, and where the husband, at
the parting, said to her, that "if she conducted herself as she ought to do
"she should not want for anything," his bill of divorce was put off to that
day six months.—Lieutenant Warrall's case, Macq. H. of L. 630.

Forgiveness by the wife of the husband's adultery on a promise of amendment. Should he again go wrong the previous injury revives.—Durant v.
Durant, 1 Hagg. Ecc. 745.

In an unreported case, Worsley v. Worsley, the counsel for the husband
admitted that fresh acts of cruelty would revive the former acts of cruelty,
but contended that, inasmuch as no fresh adultery was averred, the articles
relating to adultery were irrelevant, and ought to be struck out. The court,
however, clearly held, that the new acts of cruelty revived as well the acts of
dultery as the acts of cruelty. Referring to this case, Sir John Nicholl said,
"I wish a full argument on the doctrine of condonation, its principles, and
"the authorities respecting it. What takes off its effects and revives a former
"charge? Will any offence short of subsequent adultery, namely, an
"approach to adultery, set aside condonation as a bar? Will solicitation of
"chastity have that effect? Must the injury be *ejusdem generis?* Will
"cruelty revive adultery? If so, will any thing short of what would sub-
"stantively and separately establish a case of cruelty? Will an unfounded
"charge of adultery, of which there is not a tittle of proof, against a mother
"with twelve living children, and an unjust dismissal of the wife from her
"husband's house, be sufficient to revive condoned adultery?"
Dr. Lushington and Dr. Dodson: "We do not find that the questions
put by the court have received judicial consideration."—Durant v. Durant,
1 Hagg. Ecc. 734.

7. RECRIMINATION.

Where it appeared that the petitioner had a woman in keeping whom he
passed off as his wife. His bill of divorce was rejected.—Major Bland's case,
Macq. H. of L. 605.

Per Dr. Bettesworth: "Where adultery is pleaded by way of recrimina-
"tion, it is not necessary to prove such strong facts as would be required
"to convict the other party."—Forster v. Forster, 1 Hagg. 144. This has
been considered loose doctrine, although it received the sanction of Lord
Stowell. See Astley v. Astley, 2 Hagg. Ecc. 714.

Per Lord Stowell: "Mrs. Proctor has accused her husband of criminal
"intercourse with Charlotte Phipps; but it appears not to have taken place
"until after the adultery of Mrs. Proctor herself had been well established.
"The question arises, has he forfeited his remedy by an incontinence proved

·" to have been subsequent to the discovery of his wife's infidelity?" Upon ·referring to Sanchez, his lordship allowed the plea of recrimination.—Proctor *v.* Proctor, 2 Hagg. 292.

But a decision apparently opposite was come to in Major Campbell's case; where it having been proposed to open matter of recrimination against the petitioner subsequent to the date of the adultery charged against the wife, the Delegates in the first place, and the House of Lords afterwards, rejected the plea.—Macq. H. of L. 591.

The wife may deny her own guilt, but at the same time say, that even if she had been guilty, the husband's conduct is a bar.—3 Hagg. Ecc. 91.

---

8. WILFUL SEPARATION.

Voluntary separation for a frivolous cause. Subsequent adultery by the wife. Bill of divorce by the husband abandoned.—Mr. Barker's case, Macq. H. of L. 634.

Where a voluntary separation had taken place for a cause palpably inadequate. Bill of divorce for subsequent adultery rejected.—Mr. Woodcock's case, Macq. H. of L. 600.

The separation may be justified.—Mr. Sullivan's case, Macq. H. of L. 637. —Lord Lismore's case, Macq. H. of L. 640.—Mr. Graham's case, Macq. H. of L. 644.

A husband and wife agree to part, and a deed is executed whereby the husband renounces the marital control, and, releasing her from conjugal duty, gives her liberty to live as she pleases. There is, moreover, a clause precluding him from suing for restitution of conjugal rights. She soon afterwards commits adultery. This case, unless strong reasons were shown to justify the separation, was without redress in Parliament. Many separations take place without deed or special agreement. These, where they involve an improper surrender of marital control, will be within the rule which forms the subject of Lord Loughborough's standing order of 28th March, 1798, Macq. H. of L. 791.—Mrs. Esten's case, Macq. H. of L. 588; Mrs. Bartellott's case, Macq. H. of L. 589.

---

9. WILFUL NEGLECT.

Per Sir W. Scott: "A husband is expected by the law to pay a due " attention to the behavour of his wife, and to give her the benefit of some " superintendence when she is placed in dangerous situations." He had sent her to Lisle, a garrison town filled with officers, remaining himself in England.—Foster *v.* Foster, 1 Hagg. Con. 144.

Per a noble Lord: "The petitioner appeared to have permitted the visits of " persons at his house under circumstances which ought to have excited sus-

" picion in a well-regulated mind, and his conduct generally, in being so fre-
" quently from home, appeared to have been marked by extreme neglect."—
Col. Clayton's case.   Macq. H. of L. 661.

In many cases where there appeared extreme negligence on the part of the
husband, the House required him to prove what his conduct had been, and
that he had used due care, diligence, and caution.—Mr. Taafe's case.
Macq. H. of L. 626.

In consequence of the House observing imputations of negligence against
the husband, evidence to rebut these imputations was required.—Mr. Dundas'
case.   Macq. H. of L. 609.

10. MISCONDUCT.

Suppose the husband to be convicted of an infamous offence, rendering it
reasonably impossible for his wife to live with him.—This, according to the
Code Napoléon, would of itself warrant a divorce.   A fortiori would it be in
the discretion of the court to refuse divorce ; for a defence may be sustained
by less than is required tó support the original complaint.   Suppose the
husband guilty, but not convicted.—Here, if the fact were recent and not
condoned, the court might perhaps hold it a bar as conducing to the adultery.   Again, suppose the husband to be an incorrigible gambler or spend-
thrift, who, bringing destitution on his wife, drives her to the streets, and so
conduces to the very act of which he complains.   When these and such
cases are brought forward, justice will be done.

11. UNREASONABLE DELAY.

It was a rule of the canon law, " Adulter accusari non potest post quin-
" quenniam."—Mule v. Mule, before the Delegates in 1710, 1 Hagg. 134.

To the wife's remedy delay is not a bar.—1 Hagg. Ecc. 740. 766.

Wife's suit for divorce dismissed in respect of very great delay in prose-
secuting.—Walker v. Walker, 2 Phill. 152.

In another case nothing had been done from 1775 till 1787.—Belcher v.
Belcher, 2 Phill. 152.

A suit of divorce, after nearly fourteen years' knowledge of the adultery,
dismissed.—A.B. v. C.D., 15 Second Ser. Scotch Ca. 976.

An affidavit by the husband to account for delay in suing.—Best v. Best,
2 Phill. 172.

The effect of delay may be got over by showing want of funds.—Coode
v. Coode, 1 Curt. 755.

12. EFFECTS OF DIVORCE, AND PROVISIONS INCIDENTAL THERETO.

By marriage settlement an estate was secured, after the death of the intended wife's father, to the intended husband and herself for their joint lives, and to the survivor for life, the ultimate fee being in the wife. She committed adultery, and was divorced by the Scotch court. On her father's death she claimed a moiety of the income. Held, that the effect of the divorce was the same as if she had died. This was decided by the late Lord Rutherford, and adhered to by the Inner House after much learned argument. Thom *v.* Thom, 14 Sec. Ser. 861. This case shows that even an antenuptial settlement does not, in Scotland, save a wife from the consequences of her defection; neither will it in France. See Code Napoléon, infra, Arts. 47, 48.

In the Countess of Macclesfield's case the marriage settlements were ordered to be produced, and a clause was prepared by the judges to indemnify the earl against her debts.—Macq. H. of L. 576. This throws light on a point adverted to, supra, p. 53, as to liability for the wife's antenuptial engagements after a sentence of divorce has been pronounced.

And it is hereby further enacted, that the several provisions, by way of jointure, pin-money, or otherwise, made for the said Lady Elizabeth, by the said indenture, and all terms of years and other remedies and powers for securing, recovering, and enforcing the same, shall, from and after the passing of this Act, cease, determine, and be absolutely null and void.

And whereas it is necessary that some provision should be made for the said Lady Elizabeth; and whereas it is reasonable that the said two several sums of 5,000*l.* and 2,000*l.* mentioned in the said indenture, should immediately, after the passing of this Act, be paid, assigned, and transferred, to the said Lady Elizabeth, her exŏrs, admŏrs, and assigns: Be it therefore enacted and declared that the said B. E. H., and also the trustees named in the said indenture, shall immediately after the passing of this Act, assign and transfer the said two several sums of 5,000*l.* and 2,000*l.*, and the securities wherein or upon which the same are and shall be invested to the said Lady Elizabeth B——. her exŏrs, admŏrs, and assigns, to and for her and their use and benefit.—Mr. H——'s Divorce Act, 1794.

Bill of divorce with a clause reciting, that in consideration of the marriage, the injured husband had secured to his wife " a yearly rentcharge of 200*l.* " for her life for her jointure;" and with a clause enacting "that the said " jointure and all remedies and powers for recovering the same should from " thenceforth cease, determine, and be absolutely void and of no effect;" and another clause enacting "that it should be lawful for the said husband, " in case he should marry again, to make such jointure or jointures upon " any future wife or wives, out of the aforesaid messuages, &c., comprised, " &c., as he might have made upon any such wife or wives, in case the " said Elizabeth (the divorced wife) were dead;" and with a further clause enacting that the injured husband "should be barred of all claim to any " lands or hereditaments, &c., and estates real, personal, and mixed, and all " ornaments and wearing apparel, and all goods and chattels which the said

" Elizabeth then enjoyed or was entitled to in possession in her own right,
" or which she might thereafter acquire," &c.   Here the wife's jointure was
cut off, and no substitute provided.—Mr. S.'s Divorce Act, 1796.   See also
C.'s Divorce Act, 31 Geo. 3. c. 68.   See also Sir Wm. A.'s case, and General
D.'s case, both in 1816.

---

13. EFFECTS OF SEPARATION.

Sir Robert Belknappe, Lord Chief Justice of England, in the reign of
Richard II., having married Sibella, an heiress, holding estates in her own
right, these were not forfeited by her husband's attainder; and, bringing an
action during his banishment for an injury done to one of them, the question
arose, whether she could sue alone.   It was adjudged that inasmuch
as her husband was incapable of joining her as a plaintiff, she had privilege of suing as a *feme sole*. — Lord Campbell's Chief Justices, vol. 1.,
p. 113.

In the year 1554 one of the petitions of the clergy in convocation to the
upper house was, "that in divorces, from bed and board, provision should
' be made that the innocent woman might enjoy such lands and goods as
" were hers before the marriage; and that it should not be lawful for the
" husband, being for his offence divorced from the said woman, to inter-
" meddle himself with the said lands or goods, unless his wife should be to
" him reconciled."—Divorce Report, p. 2.

In the year 1602 a bill to suppress adultery was read the first time; the
substance whereof was that if a woman or man were convicted of adultery,
he should lose his tenancy by courtesie, and she her tenancy in dower.
The speaker putting it to the question whether the bill should be read the
second time, the House gave a great NO; saying "away with it."— Sir
Simon D'Ewe's Parliamentary Records.

Lord Kenyon, with doubtful policy, overturned some decisions of Lord
Mansfield respecting actions by and against married women separated from
their husbands by divorce à mensâ et thoro, the rule being now laid down
that a married woman cannot bring an action or be impleaded as a feme sole
while the relation of marriage subsists,—although the common law furnished
the analogy of a married woman acquiring a separate character by the exile
of her husband or by his entering into religion.—Marshall v. Rutton, 8 T.R.
545, Lord Campbell's Chief Justices, vol. 3, p. 47.

Where the husband became a Roman priest and the wife a nun, and where
they discharged each other from their nuptial obligations, the volatile husband having afterwards renounced catholicity and reverted to his original
protestant principles, he sued his wife for restitution of conjugal rights at
Doctors' Commons.   The wife resisted, pleading, as a bar, the vows she had
taken with his sanction, and contending that they had the force and the
effect of divorce à mensâ et thoro.   The judge of the Arches Court decided

that the defence was insufficient.—1 Macq. Rep. 257. And see 7 Moore, P.C.R. 438.

---

14. EVIDENCE.

The law of England considering that there are many transactions necessarily difficult of proof, is often satisfied with the testimony of a single witness; whereas the canon law invariably requires that of two at least. Cases of adultery are, of all others, the very cases in which a *penuria testium* is most likely to occur. To require absolutely evidence of two witnesses to facts scarcely ever otherwise than secret, is, in most cases, to ensure a defeat of the suit and a denial of justice. To take a single instance of recent date, that of Evans *v.* Evans, 1 Rob. 165, which came before Sir Herbert Jenner Fust in the Arches Court of Canterbury. The proceeding was by the husband against his wife for adultery. The facts were, that having suspected his dishonour, he one day returned early from shooting, and proceeded suddenly, accompanied by a female servant, to his wife's room, where they found her in bed in the arms of her paramour. Against that person the husband in due time recovered a verdict for 500*l.* damages. The evidence of adultery in the Ecclesiastical Court depended on the testimony of the female servant. That evidence had satisfied the jury; it did not, however, satisfy the learned judge of the Ecclesiastical Court; who rested his decision not on any objection to the conduct of the husband, which had been altogether blameless, nor on any doubt as to the veracity of the witness, whose character was unimpeached, but simply and solely on this ground, that the testimony of a single witness, however positive and distinct, did not of itself constitute that full degree of proof, that *plena probatio*, required by the Ecclesiastical Courts. He therefore dismissed Mr. Evans's suit. It is said that in the case of a cardinal, the *probatio*, in order to be *plena*, must be established by no less than seven *eye* witnesses; so improbable does the canon law deem it that a member of that high order can be guilty of incontinence.

All this is corrected by the 20 & 21 Vict. c. 85, the forty-eighth section of which enacts that the rules of evidence to be observed hereafter are not to be the rules of the canon law, but those of the Superior Courts of Common Law at Westminster.

The paramour is a competent witness.—At the trial of Queen Caroline her counsel were taunted because they had not produced Bergami, the alleged paramour. Mr. Denman answered, " From the beginning of the " world, no instance is to be found of a party accused of adultery being " called as a witness to disprove it."—(Lord Brougham's Speeches, vol. 1, " p. 248.) But in Major Campbell's case (Macq. H. of L. 590) the supposed paramour voluntarily gave evidence upon a divorce bill. See also the Scotch cases of Nicolson in 1770, and Hay Marshall in 1798, where the calling of the paramour to be a witness was sanctioned by the House of Lords on appeal; and Don *v.* Don, 28th May 1848; 10 Second Series of the Court of Session Reports, 1048. Mr. Starkie (Evid. 2nd edition, vol. 1, p. 171), makes this remark, " Although a witness is not bound to answer, " yet the refusal to answer must make an unfavourable impression on the " court, since an honest man would be eager to deny the fact."

In the Scotch case of Springthorpe v. Springthorpe (15th May 1830, 8 Shaw, 751,) the paramour swore to the fact, and judgment went accordingly. In Sim v. Sim, 12 Shaw, 633, two witnesses swore that they had committed adultery with the wife, but the Scotch court thinking them unworthy of credit dismissed the husband's suit.—(2 May 1834.)

In Burgess v. Burgess, the confession of the paramour was admitted.— 2 Hagg. Con. 223.

In an action of divorce by the husband against his wife, she was charged with having committed adultery with two persons named. Meetings with these persons at night in suspicious circumstances were proved, but no direct proof of adultery. The defender, on her part, sought to adduce the alleged paramours as witnesses in her favour. The commissaries held them to be inadmissible, and this decision was adhered to by the Court of Session. On appeal to the House of Lords, however, it was reversed, the Lords holding that the socii criminis were equally competent witnesses for the defender as for the pursuer.— Marshall v. Marshall, 4 Craigie and Stuart, 72.

Per Sir W. Scott : "Confession stands high, or I should say, highest, in the scale of evidence."—Mortimer v. Mortimer, 2 Hagg. Con. 310.

Per Sir W. Scott, "The more rational doctrine is, that confession proved " to be perfectly free from all suspicion of collusion, may well be sufficient " to warrant a sentence of divorce à mensâ et thoro, though not pro " dirimendo matrimonii vinculo."—Mortimer v. Mortimer, 2 Hagg. Con. 310.

Confession by the wife in presence of the two solicitors employed, the paramour confirming. Divorce pronounced.—Springthorpe v. Springthorpe, 8 Shaw, 751.

A confession made in articulo mortis, as then apprehended, but afterwards on recovery retracted, objected to, but objection overruled.—Mortimer v. Mortimer, 2 Hagg. Con. 310.

The wife admitted that it was "too true." Per Sir William Scott : "By " this she adopts the confession, which is the same as if she had confessed it " originally herself."—Burgess v. Burgess, 2 Hagg. Con. 233.

The wife's conduct and declarations on a confession by the paramour being communicated to her are admissible evidence on behalf of the husband.— Burgess v. Burgess, 2 Hagg. Con. 233.

Testimony by a witness of the wife's oral confession of adultery received in evidence.—Macq. H. of L. 655.

Wife under the influence of delirium discloses her criminal attachment.— Lieutenant Thorndyke's case. Macq. H. of L. 650.

A letter by the wife to the husband, confessing adultery, received in evidence.—Mr. Doyley's case, Macq. H. of L. 654.

Letter by the wife to the husband's agent, on proof that it was not written in consequence of any promise or threat, received de bene esse.—Lord Cloncurry's case, Macq. H. of L. 606.

Letters written by the alleged adulterer to the wife, tendered as evidence against her, received de bene esse.—Lord Glerawley's case, Macq. H. of L. 629.

Letters written by the wife to the husband, although after the separation and adultery, were yet read to prove the happy terms which existed between the parties during their conjugal cohabitation.—Captain Wyndham's case, 3 Macq. Rep. 43.

Per Sir W. Scott: The court has a right to know the witnesses' impression and belief.—Crewe v. Crewe, 3 Hagg. Ecc. 129. The rule appears to be the same in Scotland.—King v. King, 4 Sec. Ser. 590.

An observing French writer, speaking of crim. con. proceedings, says: " The testimony of young chambermaids who are brought into open court " to tell in the face of the public all they have seen, heard, or guessed at, is " a sort of prostitution."—M. Simond, vol. 1, p. 45.
The above remark was quoted in debate by Lord Lyndhurst.

The French are our superiors in delicacy. Thus, they do not allow the children or descendants to be witnesses in cases of adultery. See Code Napoléon infra, Art. 22. But we have no such scruples. In a case before Dr. Lushington very young children were witnesses, the oldest only ten years of age. The learned judge said, "The court has no discretion." —Lockwood v. Lockwood, 2 Curt. 281.

It appears that in Scotland something worse than torture is used against reluctant female witnesses in cases of divorce. Thus, per the Lord Justice Clerk Hope: "The court has to protect female witnesses from intimidation, " insult, and outrage infinitely more oppressive, and, it might have been, " more fatal, than severe physical torture." Forensic bullying has been heard of in England.

CHAPTER XXVI.

FRENCH LAW OF DIVORCE AND SEPARATION

AS SETTLED BY

NAPOLEON, FIRST CONSUL, AND HIS CONSEIL D'ÉTAT.

1. PREFATORY STATEMENT.

UNDER the old rule (derived from the Roman jurisprudence) men were marriageable at fourteen, and women at twelve. But in the Conseil d'Etat, holden at Paris in 1802 and 1803, the First Consul remarked that if divorce were to be allowed, a marriage contracted so close upon childhood would have but little chance of durability. It was absurd, he said, to permit persons so young to enter into an engagement the most critical, and which ought to be the most permanent of life.

Therefore it was decreed, and is now the law of France, that no man under eighteen years complete, and no woman under fifteen years complete, can contract matrimony.

The chief rights and duties of spouses, with reference to each other, are thus tersely defined by the Civil Code :—

1. Les époux se doivent mutuellement fidélité, secours, assistance.

2. Le mari doit protection à sa femme ; la femme, obéissance à son mari.

3. La femme est obligée d'habiter avec le mari, et de le suivre partout où il juge à propos de résider ; le mari est obligé de la recevoir, et de lui fournir tout ce qui est nécessaire pour les besoins de la vie, selon ses facultés et son état.

The ancient French law expounded by Pothier allowed separation, but prohibited divorce.

The law of 20th September 1792 took exactly the opposite course ; for it allowed divorce, but prohibited separation. Herein it concurred with the English Reformatio Legum Ecclesiasticarum.

The law of 1803, usually called the Civil Code, or Code Napoléon, allowed the *two* remedies, at the option of the parties. The advocates of divorce had nearly succeeded in excluding separation; but the First Consul and his Conseil d'Etat (remembering that the great majority of the French were Roman Catholics, who could not conscientiously accept divorce) ultimately determined to allow separation.

Divorce, however, received the first and largest attention. It occupies four elaborate chapters of the Code; whereas what is set down for separation is but a single and meagre chapter of six short articles.

The law of 8th May 1816 (at the instigation of the clergy) abolished divorce. It retained separation; not however by reviving the law as laid down by Pothier, but by leaving untouched the Civil Code of 1803, except in so far as that Code allowed divorce. Thus, the separations which now take place in France are all under the law of Napoleon.

Of that law, as promulgated in 1803, we propose to give the provisions; paying little regard to the hasty legislation of Louis XVIII., though not overlooking it.

The following are the Articles respecting Divorce.—(Art. 229—233.)

2. CAUSES OF DIVORCE.

1. The husband may demand divorce by reason of the adultery of his wife.

2. The wife may demand divorce by reason of the adultery of her husband, when he has kept his concubine in the common residence (a).

(a) This is not new, "Si quis in eâ domo in quâ cum suâ conjuge manet, con-"temnens eam cum aliâ inveniatur." Cod. lib. 5. t. 17. l. 8. de repudiis; Novell. 22. c. 15. s. 1; Novell. 117. c. 9. s. 5. The words of the Code Pénal are a little different from the above text, "The husband who shall h ve maintained a concubine in the "conjugal residence." As to the import of this law a good many questions have arisen, not only on applications for divorce, but also, and perhaps more frequently, on applications for separation; such as, quid, if the spouses residing generally in town, the husband keeps his concubine in a hou e in the country, or vice versâ; or, quid, if the husbar d ! eeps his conc bine in a "pavillon" at the end of his garden, or in an upper story while he and his family reside below "au premier;" or in the same floor, but with different doors: or put the case, that the spouses occupy a château, with a farm-house adjoining, and the husband maintains culpable relations with the farmer's daughter. All these instances are viewed by the French jurists with the strongest condemnation as colourable evasions of the law which seeks to guard the wife against the "spectacle of an odious rivalry, tending to brave and "lower her before her children and domestics in that sanctuary to the repose of which "purity is indispensable." On the other hand, the French law, though regarding the husband's adultery in all circumstances as extremely reprehensible, yet distinguishes where his infidelities are "accidental and fugitive." The French law does not encourage the wife to be a spy over her husband's actions out of doors, carrying, by her suspicions and jealousies, disquietude and misery into other families. Divorce, moreover, was never meant to be imperative, but optional with the party aggrieved. Where the wife can forgive, she ought to forgive. Her husband, as the wise and good but rough Dr. Johnson says, can impose no bastards upon her. The French Code and the English moralist concur. Every adultery by the wife is for the French husband a cause of divorce in whatever place it has been committed, and without distinguishing whether it is an accident or "des relations suivies."

3. The spouses may reciprocally demand divorce by reason of outrage, cruelty, or grave injuries (b).

(b) Les époux pourront réciproquement demander le divorce pour excès, sévices, ou injures graves de l'un d'eux envers l'autre. By "excès," French jurists mean acts of violence which endanger life. In particular, the word "excès" is interpreted to include *attentat à la vie*, i. e., an attempt by one of the spouses on the life of the other. Where established, it would seem an adequate ground for divorce. See M. Boulay, For. Cod. p. 85. The cases are not quite Utopian, even in England. By "*sévices*," French jurists mean acts of cruelty which fall short of danger to life. By "*injures graves*," French jurists mean things depending in a great degree upon the condition and mode of life of the spouses. On this head see *infrà*, French Law of Separation, p. 134.

4. The condemnation of one of the spouses to an infamous punishment shall be for the other spouse a cause of divorce.

5. The mutual and permanent agreement of the spouses, expressed in the manner prescribed by law, and after the proofs which the law requires, shall sufficiently establish that the joint life is to the parties a burthen insupportable, and that there exists a peremptory cause of divorce (*a*).

(*a*) Incompatibility of temper, though much discussed as a ground for divorce, was not admitted into the Code Napoléon. And even divorce by mutual consent was surrounded with so many impediments, guards, and restrictions that much practical mischief could scarcely have arisen from it, unless, indeed, the judges were lax, which some have said they were. Thus, the husband must have been at least twenty-five, the wife twenty-one : the marriage must have existed for two years; the divorce could not have been after twenty years, nor after the wife was forty-five; the relations must have consented; careful arrangements were required as to the children and property before the judge would pronounce sentence; and, finally, a new marriage could not be contracted until three years after the divorce. On 8th May 1816 divorce by consent was abolished, and, indeed, all other divorces. Separations by consent were *never* allowed in France.

The chapter of the Civil Code respecting divorce by mutual consent, now useless in France, and of very little value anywhere, is omitted in this statement. The discussions, however, on the subject are curious, and the remarks of the First Consul highly characteristic. His chief object in allowing divorce by consent was to veil the shame of parties in cases of adultery. It was not from any lax notions respecting marriage. On the contrary, says A. Dumas, " he early professed and practised that " strictness of principle which he preserved on the throne." See Baron Locre, Législation de la France; Jounneau and Solon; and Chauveau Adolphe; and the " Foreign Codes."

3. MACHINERY AND PROCEDURE (*b*). (Civ. Cod. 234—263.)

(*b*) The chapter on "Machinery and Procedure" illustrates the remark often made, that the French law of divorce, as settled by the Civil Code, was "liberal in principle, but meant to be strict in administration." The problem is here solved how divorces may cheaply and safely be granted to the poor. " We think it in the highest degree desirable that there should in this, as in all other matters, be the same law for the rich and the poor; so that any man, however needy, with a sufficient case, should be enabled to obtain his remedy without impediment or delay. All that is said about the danger of making divorce too easy applies exclusively to the proof required, and not to the accessibility of the tribunal. Let the conditions and the tests be rigorous, but let the courts be as open and as cheap as all courts should be."—*Times*, 15th June 1854. These sentences at first startle, but on examination are found to be little more than truisms. Sir Samuel Romilly prepared, about the year 1804, a plan of divorce for poor persons. The Commissioners were anxious to see this plan, but it could not be found among the papers left by the revered writer. He went to France when he could, and he corresponded much with Dumont. It seems probable that he had in view some adaptation of the divorce part of the Code Napoléon. See Memoirs of Romilly, vol. iii. p. 372. It is the poor who chiefly require divorce. The gentry in Scotland scarcely ever ask it, though it is there open to all. There are two ways of withholding divorce from the poor. One is to say so in words; another is to erect an unapproachable tribunal. The rich have other resources.

K

6. Whatever may be the nature of the facts or of the delinquencies which give cause for the claim of divorce, that claim must be made in the court of the arrondissement in which the spouses shall have their domicile.

7. If any of the facts alleged by the spouse demandant give cause for a criminal prosecution, the action of divorce shall remain suspended until the judgment of the Court of Assize, after which it may be resumed; and it shall not be competent to deduce from such judgment any prejudicial exception against the spouse demandant.

8. Every claim of divorce shall detail the facts. Such claim shall be carried, with the documents supporting it, if there be any such, to the judge having jurisdiction, by the spouse demandant in person, unless prevented by sickness, in which case, upon his or her request, and upon the certificate of two doctors of medicine or surgery, or of two officers of health, the judge shall repair to the residence of the demandant, and receive the application.

9. The judge, after having heard the demandant, and after having made such observations as to him may appear fit, shall mark the claim and documents, and make up a record of the whole matter. That record shall be signed by the judge and by the demandant; but in case the demandant cannot write, such fact shall be set forth by the judge on the record.

10. The judge shall write an order at the bottom of the record, requiring the parties to appear before him on a day and at an hour to be fixed by him, and for that purpose a copy of his order shall be addressed by him to the party against whom the divorce is demanded.

11. On the appointed day, the judge shall address to the two spouses, if they be present, or to the demandant if the demandant alone is present, such remarks and representations as in his judgment may bring about a reconciliation (a). But if this appear impracticable, the judge shall draw up a record, and shall make an order for the communication of the claim and of the documents supporting it to the public officer (b), and shall refer the cause to the court at large.

(a) In many cases the arguments and remonstrances of a Judge, addressed to parties under such circumstances, would put an end to the proceeding. See "Working of the present Law," infrà, p. 136.

(b) Ministre Public, Commissaire du Gouvernement, or Procureur Impérial. This public officer is to watch and stipulate for the public interest, that is to say, the general interest of families, spouses, and children. He is to examine and weigh the allegations and the evidence. He is to verify the sincerity of the parties, and to guard the court against all fraudulent collusions, concerts, and surprises. Where the defendant does not appear, the court relies on the public officer. The House of Lords has similar aid in peerage questions, and the Court of Chancery in charity cases. The Scotch, too, have their public officer—the Lord Advocate, with his learned deputies; and every market town in Scotland has its procurator fiscal, claiming descent from the Roman empire. The course of proceeding in France calls in the public officer to give his "conclusions" to the court before the court decides. His interposition is not at all confined to matters of divorce and separation, or to cases of a public kind.

12. The court, on duly considering the report of the judge, and upon hearing the opinion of the public officer, shall grant or suspend an allowance of citation.

13. The demandant, when an allowance of citation is granted by the court, shall cause the defendant to be cited in the ordinary form to appear

in person before the court, which shall sit by legal adjournment for the purpose, with closed doors (a); and the demandant shall prefix to the citation a copy of the claim of divorce, and of the documents supporting it.

(a) It would seem that the policy on which the Conseil d'Etat went was to hope for a reconciliation of the parties. Hence, down to a certain stage, the proceedings were more or less confidential. See further *infrà*, Art. 27, and note thereto.

14. At the appointed time, pursuantly to the adjournment, whether the defendant appear or not, the demandant in person (assisted by counsel, if he or she think proper) shall state the grounds of the claim, explain the documents which support it, and specify the witnesses whom he or she proposes to call.

15. If the defendant appear in person, or by attorney duly authorized, he or she may state or cause to be stated his or her observations as well on the motives of the claim as on the documents produced by the demandant, and the witnesses by him or her named. The defendant shall name on his or her side the witnesses whom he or she proposes to call; and with respect to whom the demandant in turn shall make reciprocal observations.

16. A record of the appearances, remarks, and suggestions of the parties, and of the confessions on either side, shall be made up. A reading of such record shall be given to the parties, who shall be required to sign the same; and the record shall state expressly the fact of their signature, or of their declaration that they cannot or do not choose to sign.

17. The court shall then adjourn the cause to a public hearing, for which the court will fix a day and hour, ordering the procedure to be communicated to the public officer by the reporting judge.

18. On the day and at the hour appointed, on the report of the judge, the public officer assisting, the court shall in the first place make up its mind on any objections advanced against the proceeding. In case these shall be found conclusive, the claim of Divorce shall be rejected. In the contrary case, or if no objection has been advanced, the claim of divorce shall be admitted (b).

(b) That is to say, the suit shall be allowed to proceed.

19. Immediately after the order admitting the claim of divorce, on the report of the judge, the public officer assisting, the court shall dispose of the claim, if it appears to be in a state fit for determination; if not, the court shall admit the demandant to prove such pertinent (c) facts as he or she alleges, and the defendant to the contrary proof.

(c) The order must define what facts shall be deemed " pertinent."

20. As soon as the judgment ordering the proofs has been pronounced, the registrar shall read aloud that part of the record which contains the nomination of the witnesses whom the parties propose to call (d).

(d) The giving notice who are to be the witnesses is most proper. This, however, is never attended to in the House of Lords, or in the House of Commons, when dealing with Divorce Bills. Lord Brougham well remembers the surprises of which complaints were made in the *Talbot case*, Session 1856, complaints, though fruitless, not yet discontinued. See the Duchess of Norfolk's petition to have " the names of the witnesses against her." Macq. H. of L. 565.

21. The parties shall forthwith state their respective exceptions against the witnesses. The court shall decide on these exceptions after having heard the public officer.

22. The relations of the parties (but not their children or descendants) (a) are competent witnesses; so likewise are domestics; but the court shall exercise a reasonable caution in receiving depositions from relations and domestics.

(a) This seems well discriminated. On the 13th December 1856, at the trial of an action for criminal conversation before Lord Chief Justice Cockburn and a jury, the adultery of the wife was established by the evidence of two witnesses, her daughter, a girl of seventeen, and her son, a boy of fifteen, who were put by the father into the box, to prove their mother's shame.

23. Every order admitting a proof testimonial shall mention the witnesses to be examined, and fix the day and hour for the parties to present them.

24. The depositions of witnesses shall be received by the court (b) sitting *with closed doors*, in presence of the public officer, of the parties, and of their counsel or friends to the number of three on each side.

(b) Although the evidence is in the form of written deposition, yet the proceeding is not before an examiner or commissioner, but before the court itself.

25. The parties shall be at liberty, by themselves or their counsel, to address to the witnesses such remarks and interpellations as they may judge proper, without, however, interrupting the course of the depositions.

26. Each deposition shall be reduced to writing, as well as the remarks and observations to which they may give rise. The record of the proof shall be read as well to the witnesses as to the parties. and both shall be required to sign the record, which shall make mention of their signature, or of their declaration that they cannot or will not sign.

27. At the close of the two proofs, or of that of the demandant, if the defendant has not produced witnesses, the court shall adjourn the cause to a public hearing (c), for which it shall appoint a day and hour. It shall order the communication of the procedure to the Public Officer, appointing one of the judges to report.

(c) The taking of the evidence is not open to the general public; only the professional men (if such are employed) and a friend or two, with the parties, are allowed to be present. (Art. 24.) But the argument and judgment are in open court. The question is, whether this partial secresy has not two considerable advantages, which probably weighed with Napoleon and his Council: 1st, The protection of the nation from the contaminating example of domestic immoralities; and, 2nd, The saving of the unhappy parties and their relatives from an unnecessary exposure and humiliation, the dread of which would often forbid resort to the remedy of divorce, even in cases of the greatest hardship and cruelty. (See the opinion of M. Boulay in the " Foreign Codes.") In England there is a horror, generally a just horror, of closed doors in all judicial proceedings; but yet, every now and then, we have applications made to a judge to hear and dispose of a particular case in private, and no one suggests that such applications are improperly complied with. This is a question for the Legislature. See *suprà*, Art. 13. and note.

28. On the day fixed for the definitive judgment the report shall be made by the judge appointed. The parties may then make, either by themselves or their counsel, such observations as they may deem useful to their cause ; after which the public officer shall deliver his opinion.

29. The definitive judgment shall be pronounced publicly ; when it decrees divorce, the demandant shall be empowered to repair to the officer of the civil state to get the decree promulgated.

30. When the claim of divorce shall be made on the ground of outrage, cruelty, or grave injuries, although it may be well established, yet the judges cannot immediately decree the divorce. Before pronouncing judgment, they shall direct the wife to quit the company of her husband, without being obliged to receive him unless she think proper ; and they shall order the

husband to pay her an alimentary allowance, suitable to his means, if the wife has not herself sufficient income to supply her wants.

31. After one year, if the parties are not re-united, the spouse demandant may cause the other spouse to be cited to appear before the court, in order to hear definitive judgment pronounced, from thenceforth absolutely decreeing the divorce (a).

(a) This suspende1 divorce is called by M. Boulay, Séparation d'épreuve. " Foreign Codes," p. 85.

32. When the divorce shall be claimed on the ground that one of the spouses is condemned to an infamous punishment, the sole formalities to be observed shall consist of presenting to the Court of the First Instance a formal exemplification of the condemnation, with a certificate from the Court of Assize that the condemnation is no longer liable to be altered in any legal manner.

33. In the event of an appeal from the judgment admitting the claim of divorce, or from the definite judgment delivered by the Court of First Instance, in the matter of divorce, the cause shall be taken up and disposed of by the Cour Royale out of the ordinary course, as an affair of urgency.

34. The appeal shall not be receivable unless asserted within three months.

4. PROVISIONAL MEASURES PENDENTE LITE. (Civ. Cod. 267-271.)

35. The care of the children, pending the proceedings, shall remain with the husband, whether demandant or defendant, at least till the court shall otherwise order, which it may do on the application of the mother, or of the family, or of the public officer, having regard to what shall appear most for the benefit of the children.

36. The wife, demandant or defendant, may quit the residence of the husband pending the proceedings, and may demand an alimentary allowance corresponding with the husband's means. The court shall prescribe the residence in which the wife shall remain, and shall fix, if necessary, the alimentary allowance which the husband shall be obliged to pay to her.

37. The wife shall be bound to prove her residence in the appointed place as often as she shall be called upon so to do ; and in the event of her failing to give a proper account of herself, the husband may withhold his alimentary allowance; and if she is the demandant of divorce he may move to have it declared that she is not to be at liberty to continue her suit.

38. To protect her rights, in the case of communio bonorum (b), the wife whether demandant or defendant, may at every stage of the cause (from the date of the order mentioned in Article 10) require the affixing of seals to the moveable effects, which seals shall not be taken off except in making the inventory by appraisement, the husband being bound to produce the articles inventoried, or to account for their value, as judicial custodier thereof.

(b) As to the Communio Bonorum, or Régime de Communauté, see infrà, p. 137.

39. All obligations contracted by the husband affecting the goods in communion, and every alienation of immoveables connected therewith, subsequently to the date of the order mentioned in Article 10, shall be pronounced void, if it appear that the same shall have been executed in fraud of the rights of the wife.

5. Effects of Reconciliation. (Civ. Cod. 272—274.)

40. The action of divorce shall be extinguished by the supervening reconciliation of the spouses, whether subsequent to the facts which might have authorized the action, or subsequent to the claim of divorce.

41. In either case the demandant shall be pronounced not at liberty to proceed in the action; the demandant, however, may commence a new action for cause given subsequently to the reconciliation, and may then make use of the old grounds in support of the new claim.

42. If the demandant denies the reconciliation, the defendant may prove it by writing or by witnesses.

6. Effects of Divorce. (Civ. Cod. 295—301.)

43. The divorced spouses can never afterwards be re-united (a).

(a) In the event of children by second marriages, there would be something unseemly in a re-conjunction. The provision is to meet a thing not likely to happen.

44. The divorced wife cannot re-marry until ten months after the sentence of divorce (b).

(b) The old English law decently forbade a woman to re-marry till the expiration of a year—the annus luctûs. This was also a Roman regulation. The reason for the ten months in France is to get over gestation. See chap. 8, supra p. 46.

45. In the case of divorce for adultery, the guilty spouse can never marry the accomplice.

46. The wife guilty of adultery shall, upon the requisition of the public officer, be condemned to confinement in a house of correction for a fixed term, which cannot be less than three months nor more than two years (c).

(c) It is in the husband's power to remit this. See infrà, " Of Separations," Art. 4. p. 134, and " Punishment of Adultery," Art. 2. p. 139.

47. The spouse against whom the divorce is decreed shall lose all the advantages which the other spouse may have conferred, whether by the contract of marriage, or since the date of the marriage.

48. The spouse obtaining the divorce shall preserve all the advantages on him or her conferred by the other spouse, although such advantages were the result of reciprocal stipulations, and the reciprocity has not been made good (d).

(d) This is unsatisfactorily rendered, and it is best to give the original. "L'époux " qui aura obtenu le divorce conservera les avantages à lui faits par l'autre époux, " encore qu'ils aient été stipulés reciproques, et que la réciprocité n'ait pas lieu."

49. If the spouses have not respectively conferred advantages on each other, or if the advantages stipulated for shall not appear sufficient to secure the subsistence of the spouse who has obtained the divorce, the court may award to such spouse, out of the property of the other spouse, an alimentary allowance, which must not exceed a third part of the income of such other spouse. That allowance shall be revocable when it shall cease to be necessary.

50. The children shall be confided to the spouse who has obtained the divorce; unless the court, on the application of the family, or of the public officer, shall order, for the greater advantage of the children, that all, or some of them, be confided to the care either of the other spouse, or of a third person.

51. Whosoever the person be to whom the children are confided, the father and mother shall respectively retain the right of superintending the bringing up and education of their children, and shall be bound to contribute to that end according to their means (a).

(a) The French wife is bound to apply her separate property to the maintenance of the family. An English wife is under no such obligation. See case mentioned *infrà*, p. 139.

52. The dissolution of the marriage by divorce shall not deprive the children born of that marriage of any of the advantages secured to them by law, or by the matrimonial conventions of the father and mother; but there shall be no acceleration of the rights of the children, except in the same manner, and under the same circumstances as if there had been no divorce.

7. JUDICIAL SEPARATION, AS SETTLED BY THE FIRST CONSUL AND THE CONSEIL D'ETAT, NOW IN FORCE.

Séparation de corps indicates the position of spouses legally released from the obligation of living together.

Very different from divorce, this separation leaves unbroken the tie of marriage, and only modifies its duties.

Four distinct epochs are to be distinguished in the history of this branch of French law:—

1. The ancient jurisprudence, which, in conformity with the Popish dogma, proclaimed the absolute indissolubility of marriage, prohibiting divorce, and permitting only separation. (Poth. de Con. de Mar., Nos. 462, 466.)

2. The legislation of the 20th September 1792 (S. 1., Art. 17.), prohibiting separation, and permitting only divorce; and founded not a little on our own Reformatio Legum Ecclesiasticarum, the great work of Cranmer.

3. The Civil Code, or Code Napoleon, (decreed 21st March 1803,) which authorized at once both divorce and separation; and

4. Finally, the law of the restoration, carried by the clergy on the 8th May 1816, under which there remains now only the séparation de corps, by which is meant such parts of the Code Napoléon as allow what in England would be called separation from bed and board, as granted by the Ecclesiastical Courts.

At one time the advocates of divorce in the Conseil d'Etat had nearly succeeded in excluding separation entirely, as had been the case under the law of 20th September 1792; but, in the end, separation was held indispensable, regard having been had to the fact, that the great majority of the French nation were of the Roman Catholic faith, by which divorce is forbidden. Hence separation and divorce were admitted in the same Code, and for the same causes, both remedies being offered to the free choice of the spouses. (See Locré, Legisl. Civ. t. 5., pp. 3. 131. 142.)

Unfortunately the authors of the Civil Code neglected to define the parallel which they established between divorce and separation, the First Consul observing that divorce engaged at the outset their chief consideration; and after having devoted to it no less than four very extended chapters, the framers of the Code threw into a single chapter, consisting of only six articles, the whole matter relating to separation.

The inconvenience would have been less had the framers indicated by reference the articles respecting divorce which they intended to apply to separation. This, in truth, they did with respect to some few of them; but they thereby made the doubts and embarrassments only the more puzzling as to other articles not similarly discriminated.

The chapter of the Civil Code applicable to separations can be made complete only by incorporating into it the corresponding provisions of divorce fitted to the circumstances; but divorce and separation being things in some respects resembling, in others widely differing from, each other, it is to be regretted that the First Consul and his able coadjutors did not more clearly mark the limits of that analogy which generally guides, but sometimes perplexes, the Courts.

8. THE FOLLOWING ARE THE ARTICLES OF THE CIVIL CODE RESPECTING SEPARATIONS. (Civ. Cod. 306—311.)

1. In cases where there is ground for the claim of divorce it is allowable to claim separation (a).

(a) The cases which give "ground for the claim of divorce" are stated, *ante*, pp. 128 and 129. The French judges are represented as singularly circumspect and wary, and reluctant to interpose. They are the jury. The legislature has given a wide range to their wisdom, discernment, and experience. Perhaps this is better than a parade of restrictive definitions. Lord Campbell has lately affirmed that the best part of English law is that which the judges have made.

In dealing with claims for *Séparation de Corps* on the ground of ill-treatment a French text writer (M. Demolombe) observes: The injuries must be considerable. Outbreaks of temper and harsh words are not regarded—where is the family without these? The court will consider whether the act is accidental; whether it is public or private, having regard to its nature and all the circumstances; how far there has been provocation; what has been the education of the parties, their habits, their social position. Thus, a blow of the fist, which in the humbler ranks is followed by reprisals and instantly forgotten, will, if administered in a higher station, prove for ever fatal to conjugal repose. The ages of the parties must likewise be adverted to, the court being slow to separate those who have scarcely had time to know each other; and, perhaps, still more reluctant to dissolve a tie cemented by long years of common habits and reciprocal toleration. Finally, and above all, says the French law, the court is to see whether there are children of the marriage. Having regard to these particulars, M. Demolombe tell us, that a calumnious accusation of adultery made by a husband against his wife, especially if made publicly, with precision, and designating with whom; the inflexible refusal of the husband to receive his wife in the conjugal residence, or of the wife to return thither (which in England would be a case for restitution of conjugal rights): the communication of a noxious disease; the discovery that the wife was unchaste before the marriage; all these seem grounds for séparation de corps. But neither reverse of fortune, nor physical or moral infirmities, nor fatuity, nor madness, nor maladies the most contagious and disgusting, no calamity, in short, no misfortune of the one spouse shall be to the other a cause of separation.

2. Separation shall be sued for, established, and adjudged in the same manner as any other civil action. It cannot take place by the mutual consent of the spouses.

3. The wife against whom separation is pronounced by reason of adultery shall be condemned by the same judgment, and, on the requisition of the public officer, to confinement in a house of correction for a term not less than three months nor more than two years (b).

(b) Nov. 117. c. 8. s. 1. Cod. Leg. de Adulteriis. See "Punishment of Adultery," Articles 1 and 2, *suprà*, p. 139.

4. The husband shall have the power of superseding the effect of that condemnation, by consenting to take his wife back (a).

(a) Nov. 134. c. 10. See "Punishment of Adultery," Articles 1 and 2, infra, p. 140.

5. When the separation (pronounced for any other cause than the adultery of the wife) shall have lasted three years, the spouse who was originally defendant may claim divorce; and the court shall admit the demand if the original demandant does not at once put an end to the separation (b).

(b) This, seems consistent enough with the other provisions of the Code; the Conseil d'Etat probably holding that spouses who continued apart for three years under a sentence of separation pronounced for something short of adultery, had better be divorced at once, and that the original defendant might, under such circumstances, turn round on the original demandant.

6. Separation of the person shall always import separation of the property (c).

(c) This article refers back to the article, ante, p. 7: " Les époux se doivent mutuellement fidélité, secours, assistance," as furnishing the principle. It then cites Article 49, ante, p. 134, as furnishing the measure.

9. WORKING OF THE PRESENT LAW IN FRANCE.

The Minister of Justice, in his recent Report to the Emperor, states, that of the cases submitted to the French tribunals, those for séparation de corps are rather on the decline; for that in 1853 the number of them was 1,722, whereas in 1854 the number was but 1,681.

Of the 1,681 cases which came before the courts of France in 1854, those for—

Ill-treatment were	1,410
Those for adultery by the wife	116
Those for adultery by the husband	109
Those for condemnations to infamous punishments	46
	1,681

Out of these it appears that 1,510 were by wives and 171 by husbands. 1,242 were received or admitted, 174 were rejected, while the remaining 265 were abandoned on the reconciliation of the parties, most probably effected by the happy influence of judicial authority and advice so wisely prescribed by the Code (d).

(d) See suprà, p. 130, Arts. 11 and 13.

The moral spectacle presented by these returns is not very depressing, the greatness of the French population considered. The total number of suits for separation, after deducting those rejected and those compounded, is 1,242. Only 225 are for adultery. The others, amounting to 1,017, are for outrages, cruelty, and penal misconduct. The question is, does the like or a greater number of similar delinquencies occur every year in England? or even in the metropolis alone?

An ingenious writer (e) remarks, after a keen inspection, that the absolute indissolubility of the marriage tie operates immorally in France, preventing marriage itself, the parent of all order. "Matrimony," he observes, "once " entered into, can never be dissolved, whatever causes of misery may arise. " The severity of the statute doubtless has its weight in producing the too " general state of concubinage."

(e) Mr. Jarves' Parisian Sights and French Principles seen through American Spectacles.

Beyond all controversy, the great blot on the legislation of 1803 was the allowance of divorce by mutual consent.

In other respects the Code Napoléon was wise and beneficial, and we have reason to believe that its restoration would be hailed with satisfaction by all who, denying the doctrine of indissolubility, are of opinion that mere separation, without divorce, is no adequate redress for adultery when committed by the wife, and that it sometimes works mischievously. "Notwithstanding " the sentence, she retains her husband's name, and dishonours it. Respect " for religious scruples compels us to admit séparation de corps; but that " legislation *must* be immoral which permits a wife guilty of adultery to go " and live with her seducer (a)."

(a) Per the First Consul, See " Foreign Codes, pp. 33, 38, 40.

Two attempts were made to re-establish the Civil Code in France; one in 1830, and another in 1848. Both were unsuccessful.

10. French Wife's Position as to Property and Earnings—Her Protective Remedies.

In one respect a French wife enjoys by law a superiority over an English one; for a French wife can make a will (b), which an English one cannot.

(b) It is expressly enacted that she can " test," that is, make her last will and testament, " without authorization from her husband."

But, as a general rule, a French wife can do nothing of herself. She can neither give, nor lend, nor borrow, nor alienate, nor mortgage, nor contract, nor transact, nor acquire anything; nor can she sue or be sued civilly in any court of justice. As her husband's agent she binds him, but not herself.

Much learning and ingenuity are expended by the French jurists in explaining the principle of the husband's dominion and of the wife's subjugation and consequent disability. The fact is enough for the present purpose.

Parties intending to intermarry in France may declare beforehand whether they mean that their union shall be under the Régime de Communauté or under the Régime Dotal.

We are told that ninety-nine per cent. of all French marriages are entered into en Communauté.

By this Régime de Communauté all the moveable property of both parties is thrown into a common stock, managed by the husband by virtue of his marital prerogative. He may, unless restrained, squander the whole of it during the coverture, but he can bequeath only his own proportion.

The wife's immoveable property remains with her under the Régime de Communauté, but the income and administration are the husband's.

All this corresponds with the law now existing in Scotland, where the communio bonorum and jus relictæ furnish daily occupation for the courts.

The Régime Dotal, or, more properly, the Régime de Dot et des Biens paraphernaux, has for its object to protect the wife, and peradventure, the husband himself, and the family, from the consequences of his improvidence, ill luck, or misconduct, under a law which gives him a power almost unlimited over her person and her estate; a power, however, liable to be curbed, as will appear presently.

Both Régimes are old contrivances. The Roman law had them. The separate property of the Roman wife was called her parapherna, or peculium.

It might consist of moveable or immoveable property of any description or amount. What passed to the husband by the marriage was the dos or dowry. But how thoroughly the husband was excluded from intermeddling with the parapherna, appears from the following strong mandate of Justinian:—"Decernimus ut vir, in his quas extra dotem mulier habet, nullam " habeat communionem, uxore prohibente, nec aliquam ei necessitatem " imponat. Quamvis enim bonum erat mulierum quæ seipsam marito " committit, res etiam ejusdem pari arbitrio gubernari, attamen nullo modo, " muliere prohibente, virum in paraphernis se volumus emiscere."

Blackstone says, that parapherna "meant something over and above the " widow's dower;" as if she were to gain something in addition to her dower out of her husband's estate at his death. Whereas in the Roman law, and (as we shall see) also in the French law, it meant something of her own, not surrendered by her at the marriage,—something reserved and kept back from the dos or fortune which she brought her husband (a).

(a) Macqueen on the Rights and Liabilities of Husband and Wife, p. 151.

On turning to Article 1540 of the Civil Code, we find these words :—" La " dot est le bien que la femme apporte au mari pour supporter les charges " du mariage." And on turning to Article 1574 we find these words:— " Tous les biens de la femme qui n'ont pas été constitué en dot, sont para- " phernaux." This shows how closely the Roman law has been adhered to by Napoleon and his Conseil d'État.

The dos is managed by the husband; but neither he, nor his wife, nor himself and his wife together, can alienate it, for it is to support the family. The wife, however, with his consent, may make advancements out of it for the establishment of the children.

On the dissolution of the marriage there will be a claim of restitution of the dos.

The paraphernal effects are liable to contribute towards the maintenance of the family, and herein they differ from the separate property created by English courts of equity. Furthermore, although the wife has the enjoyment of her paraphernal property, she cannot alienate it without the husband's consent. And here again is another point of difference from the English Separate Use which is vested in the wife as a femme sole absolutely (b).

(b) The separate estate of an English wife she may keep accumulating at interest, while her husband and family are without bread ; or she may elope, and bestow all on her paramour. This happened some years ago, in a remarkable case, finally determined by the House of Lords. See *Hodgens* v. *Hodgens*, 4 Cla. & Finn. 323.

Without submitting themselves to the Régime Dotal, parties may declare that they are to be séparés des biens; but no convention or stipulation will enable the wife to alienate her immoveable property without the marital or judicial authority.

From all this it rather appears that the marital sovereignty prevails more or less throughout the matrimonial system of France, whatever régime or modification be resorted to. The wife consequently is subject to an incapacity which fetters or paralyses her at every turn.

But she can have redress under the French law when she needs and demands it. In order to take off her incapacity, she may obtain what is called authorization; this may be given by the husband. Should he refuse, or be unable to grant it, the wife is at liberty to apply to the court of the arrondissement, which, on cause shown, will grant a judicial authorization.

By virtue of authorization, the wife becomes as capable as if she had not been married. This is expressly laid down (a).

(a) " L'effet général de l'autorisation accordée à la femme, soit par son mari, soit " par la justice, est de lever l'incapacité qui résultait pour elle de l'état de mariage. " La femme autorisée-devient donc aussi capable, ni plus ni moins, que si elle n'était " pas mariée."—Demolombe, Du Mar. et de la Séparation de Corps, vol. 2, p. 364. Art. 218 of the Civil Code enacts, " Si le mari refuse d'autoriser sa femme à estre en " jugement, le juge peut donner l'autorisation." Estre en jugement is a phrase borrowed from the Roman law : Stare in judicio It has not been found that these appeals to justice disturb domestic happiness. A washerwoman was called upon to pay a debt of her husband's out of her earnings. She applied to the court, which gave her at once an order of protection. This was accomplished in the course of a morning in August 1856.

And although it is said that there cannot be a separation of the person without a separation of the property, yet there may be a separation of the property without a separation of the person. Thus, even under the Régime de Communauté (which is less favourable to the wife than the Régime Dotal), if the husband takes to squandering, she can insist on a division of the moveable property, and have the administration of her own fortune committed to herself.

The Report of the Minister of Justice, already cited, informs the Emperor that the number of claims for séparation des biens disposed of in 1854 was 4,293, and that of these only 1,281 were rejected.

11. Adultery a Crime in France.
Punishment thereof under the Code Napoleon.
(Pen. Cod., 336–340.)

1. The adultery of the wife can be denounced by the husband only, and even his power shall cease if the case comes within Article 4, infrà.

2. The wife convicted of adultery shall undergo the penalty of imprisonment for a period not less than three months nor more than two years. The husband shall continue entitled to stop the effect of that condemnation, he consenting to take his wife back.

3. The accomplice of a wife guilty of adultery shall be punished by imprisonment during the same space of time, and subject besides to a fine of from 100 to 2,000 francs.

4. The husband who shall have maintained a concubine in the conjugal residence, and who shall be convicted on the complaint of his wife (a), shall be punished by a fine of from 100 to 2,000 francs.

(a) Divorce is not publici juris. Marriage is. Divorce is a private remedy. Therefore, in cases of adultery, the public prosecution must be backed by the private instigation. If the injured party submits, no one else can complain. Adultery is, in its nature, rather a sin than a crime. The legal point is thus put by Mr. Commissary Todd : " In certain circumstances," he observes, " the dissolution of the marriage contract is indeed permitted ; but the law of divorce in Scotland, is barely permissive, not imperative. It tolerates what it neither commands nor approves."—Ferg. Con. Dec. 316. This view is now adopted by the Legislature, which has refused to impose a fine on adultery, or to annex any punishment to it.

12. COMMUNICATION
FROM THE FRENCH MINISTER OF JUSTICE.

On the 1st January, 1857, the Honorary Secretary had the honour of receiving the following courteous note from his Excellency the Ambassador of France :—

" L'Ambassadeur de France présente ses compliments à Monsieur
" J. Fraser Macqueen, et en réponse à la demande qu'il a addressée à
" M. le Ministre de la Justice à Paris, il a l'honneur de lui transmettre
" ci-joint trois volumes * des comptes rendus de la Justice Civile et
" Commerciale en France pour les années 1850, 1853, et 1854. Quant
" à ceux pour 1855 et 1856 M. Abbatucci † annonce qu'ils n'ont
" pas encore été publiés."
" Albert Gate House, 26 Décembre, 1856."

The following are extracts from the Reports of the Minister of Justice in so far as the same relate to Séparations de Corps and Separation de Biens :—

13. REPORT TO THE PRESIDENT OF THE REPUBLIC,
13 *November*, 1852.

Séparations de Corps.

Durant les années 1841 à 1850, les tribunaux civils ont eu à connaître de 10,616 demandes en séparation de corps. Le nombre moyen annuel est donc de 1,062 ; et il a été à peu près le même de 1841 à 1845 que de 1846 à 1850. Il en est formé un bien plus grand nombre chaque année ; car, de 1846 à 1850, les présidents des tribunaux civils ont eu à s'occuper de 1,818, par année moyenne, aux termes des articles 876 et suivants du Code Napoléon. Ces magistrats en concilient à peu près un sixième dans leur cabinet, ils prononcent dans les 1,500 autres des ordonnances de renvois devant les tribunaux *par suite de non-conciliation.*

Un tiers environ de ces dernières n'y sont cependant pas portées, soit que les parties mettent à profit les conseils qu'elles ont reçus des présidents, soit faute de ressources.

Les 10,616 demandes ont été introduites, 725 seulement (7 sur 100) par les maris, et 9,891 (93 sur 100) par les femmes. Des demandes reconventionelles ont été formées dans 439 affaires ; 354 par les maris et 85 par les femmes.

---

* These interesting quarto volumes, extending to 676 pages, are now deposited in the Library of the Law Amendment Society. They contain details wonderfully laboured and minute, giving a view of municipal administration at once legal, political, and moral ; and showing, better than we have seen yet displayed, what are the great functions of a Minister of Justice. From these returns we collect that good sense and careful government are not exclusively confined to the British islands.

† Le Garde des Sceaux, Ministre de la Justice.

Dans 3,242 affaires, les époux appartenaient à des professions libérales ou vivaient de leurs revenus comme propriétaires ou rentiers ; dans 2,197 ils se livraient au commerce ; dans 1,840 ils étaient cultivateurs ; et dans 2,377, ouvriers de toute espèce.   Ce renseignement n'a pas été recueilli à l'égard de 960 affaires.

Les mariages dataient, 196 de moins d'un an ; 2,119 d'un an à cinq ans ; 2,470 de cinq ans à dix ans ; 3,168 de dix ans à vingt ans ; 1,990 de plus de vingt ans.   La durée de 678 n'a pu être indiquée.

Il était né des enfants de 5,909 mariages, plus de six dixièmes ; et 3,845 avaient été stériles.   Ce renseignement manque pour 862.

Les demandes, tant principales que reconventionelles étaient fondées, 9,718 (88 sur 100) sur des excès, sévices, ou injures graves ; 525 sur l'adultère de la femme, et 568 sur celui du mari ; 244, enfin, sur la condamnation des défendeurs à des peines afflictives et infamantes.   Ces dernières se jugent souvent sur requête.

Les tribunaux ont accueilli 7,687 demandes (876 sur 1,000) en prononçant la séparation de corps ; ils en ont rejeté 1,084 (124 sur 1,000) ; 1,845, un sixième environ du nombre total, ont été rayées des rôles par suite d'abandon ou de réconciliation des époux.

Les demandes en séparation de corps se classent d'une manière fort inégale entre les divers départements ; très rares, en général, dans les départements du Midi, elles sont, au contraire, relativement nombreuses dans les départements du Nord.

Il en a été jugé, année moyenne, 140 dans le département de la Seine, près d'un sixième du nombre total ; 29 dans le Calvados ; 26 dans la Seine-Inférieure ; 25 dans l'Eure ; 23 dans le Rhône ; 22 dans le Nord ; 21 dans Seine-et-Oise ; 20 dans la Meuse ; tandis que dans l'Ariége, les Pyrénées-Orientales, le Cantal, la Corse, les Landes, l'Ardèche, les Basses-Alpes, la Corrèze, Tarn-et-Garonne, l'Aude, l'Aveyron, l'Allier, il n'y en a eu qu'une ou deux par année.

Demandes en Séparation de Biens.

Les demandes en séparation de biens seulement sont beaucoup plus fréquentes que les demandes en séparation de corps et de biens.   Leur nombre moyen annuel a été de 5,412, de 1846 à 1850 ; de 1841 à 1845, il n'avait été que de 4,127 : il a donc augmenté de 31 pour 100 en cinq ans.

Des 47, 694 demandes de séparation de biens qui ont été jugées de 1841 à 1850, il n'y en a eu que 873 de rejetées (moins de 2 pour cent.) ; 46,821 (98 sur 100) ont été accueillies.

Les créanciers des maris étaient intervenants dans 1,243 des 27,060 affaires de séparation de biens qui ont été jugées de 1846 à 1850.   Le résultat de ces 1,243 affaires a peu différé de celui des affaires jugées sans l'intervention des créanciers de maris.   En effet 96 sur 100 ont été accueillies, et 4 rejetées au lieu de 2.

Durant les dix années (1841 à 1850) les créanciers du mari ont attaqué, comme obtenus en fraude de leurs droits, 372 jugements qui prononçaient des séparations de biens.   Ils en ont fait annuler près de la moitié 181 ; et 191 on été maintenus.

Les actions en séparation de biens seulement ne varient pas moins d'un département à l'autre que les demandes en séparation de corps. C'est aussi dans le département de la Seine qu'il s'en juge le plus chaque année : 320 année moyenne, de 1846 à 1850 ; viennent ensuite l'Isère, où il y en a presque autant que dans la Seine, 315 ; le Calvados 225 ; l'Eure 189 ; la Seine-Inférieure 182 : l'Aveyron 179 ; la Drôme 176 ; la Haute-Loire 150.

Il n'y en a pas eu plus d'une par année dans la Corse ; il y en a eu 7 dans le Morbihan ; 8 dans le Finistère ; et de 11 à 20 dans les Pyrénées-Orientales, l'Ariège, la Vendée, la Mayenne, les Landes, les Côtes-du-Nord, la Haute-Marne. Les départements industriels sont en général ceux où les séparations de biens sont le plus fréquentes, et les départements agricoles ceux où l'on en compte le moins.

----

14. REPORT TO THE EMPEROR NAPOLEON III.,

7 April 1855.

SÉPARATIONS DE CORPS.

Sous l'influence de la loi relative à l'assistance judiciare, le nombre des demandes en séparation de corps portées devant les tribunaux civils a continué d'augmenter en 1853. Ces tribunaux n'avaient eu à s'occuper que de 1,191 en 1851. Le nombre s'en était élevé à 1,477 en 1852, et, en 1853, il a été de 1,722. C'est, en deux ans, une augmentation de 531, soit 43 p. %.

Sur les 1,722 demandes en séparation de corps de 1853, il y en a eu 290 de retirées par les parties qui s'étaient réconciliées, ou d'abandonnées par suite de décès de l'un des époux ou de toute autre cause ; 1,260 ont été accueillies et 172 rejetées.

Ces demandes étaient formées, 160 seulement par les maris, et 1,562 par les femmes. Elles étaient pour la plupart motivées sur des excès, sévices, ou injures graves.

DEMANDES EN SÉPARATION DE BIENS.

Le nombre des demandes en séparation de biens a, au contraire, diminué en 1853. Les tribunaux n'ont eu à statuer que sur 4,283, tandis qu'ils en avaient jugé 4,680 en 1852, et 4,775 en 1851. Le nombre s'en était même élevé à 5,310 en 1850, et à 5,874 en 1849. Ces sortes de demandes, qui ont pour objet de sauve-garder les intérêt des femmes contre les poursuites des créanciers du mari, se produisent nécessairement en plus grand nombre dans les moments de crise commerciale ou industrielle que dans le temps de prospérité.

15. REPORT TO THE EMPEROR NAPOLÉON III.
30 *April* 1856.
Séparations de Corps.

Le nombre des demandes en séparation de corps, qui n'avait pas cessé de s'accroître chaque année depuis que la loi sur l'assistance judiciaire du 22 Janvier 1851 a facilité à tous les justiciables l'accès des tribunaux, a un peu diminué en 1854. Il n'en a été introduit que 1,681, au lieu de 1,722 en 1853. En 1852, il en avait été formé 1,477 ; et 1,191 en 1851.

Les 1,681 demandes de 1854 ont été introduites : 1,510 par les femmes, et 171 par les maris. Elles étaient fondées sur la condemnation de l'un des époux à une peine afflictive et infamante ; 1,410 sur des sévices, ou injures graves ; 116 sur l'adultère de la femme ; et 109 sur celui du mari.

Les tribunaux ont accueilli 1,242 demandes de séparation, et ils en ont rejeté 174 seulement ; 265 ont été rayées des rôles par suite de réconciliation ou d'abandon.

Demandes de Séparation de Biens.

Les tribunaux qui avaient statué en 1853 sur 4,283 demandes en séparation de biens, en ont jugé 4,293 en 1854, soit 10 de plus. En 1852 et 1851, ils en avaient jugé 4,680 et 4,775 ; en 1850 et 1849, jusqu'à 5,310 et 5,874.

Toutes les demandes formées en 1854 ont été accueillies, à l'exception de 128, environ 3 sur 100.

THE DIVORCE AND MATRIMONIAL CAUSES ACT.

ANNO VICESIMO & VICESIMO PRIMO VICTORIÆ REGINÆ.

CAP. LXXXV.

An Act to amend the Law relating to Divorce and Matrimonial Causes in England. [28th *August* 1857.]

WHEREAS it is expedient to amend the Law relating to Divorce, and to constitute a Court with exclusive Jurisdiction in Matters Matrimonial in England, and with Authority in certain Cases to decree the Dissolution of a Marriage: Be it therefore enacted by the Queen's most Excellent Majesty, by and with the Advice and Consent of the Lords Spiritual and Temporal, and Commons, in this present Parliament assembled, and by the Authority of the same, as follows:

Commencement of Act.

I. This Act shall come into operation on such Day, not sooner than the First Day of January One thousand eight hundred and fifty-eight, as Her Majesty shall by Order in Council appoint, provided that such Order be made One Month at least previously to the Day so to be appointed.

Jurisdiction in Matters Matrimonial now vested in Ecclesiastical Courts to cease.

II. As soon as this Act shall come into operation, all Jurisdiction now exerciseable by any Ecclesiastical Court in England in respect of Divorces à Mensâ et Thoro, Suits of Nullity of Marriage, Suits of Jactitation of Marriage, Suits for Restitution of Conjugal Rights, and in all Causes, Suits, and Matters Matrimonial, shall cease to be so exerciseable, except so far as relates to the granting of Marriage Licences, which may be granted as if this Act had not been passed.

The Court may enforce Decrees or Orders made before this Act comes into operation.

III. Any Decree or Order of any Ecclesiastical Court of competent Jurisdiction which shall have been made before this Act comes into operation, in any Cause or Matter Matrimonial, may be enforced or otherwise dealt with by the Court for Divorce and Matrimonial Causes herein-after mentioned, in the same Way as if it had been originally made by the said Court under this Act.

As to Suits pending when this Act comes into operation.

IV. All Suits and Proceedings in Causes and Matters Matrimonial which at the Time when this Act comes into operation shall be pending in any Ecclesiastical Court in England shall be transferred to, dealt with, and decided by the said Court for Divorce and Matrimonial Causes as if the same had been originally instituted in the said Court.

Power to Judges whose Jurisdiction is determined to deliver written Judgments.

V. Provided, That if at the Time when this Act comes into operation any Cause or Matter which would be transferred to the said Court for Divorce

L.

and Matrimonial Causes under the Enactment herein-before contained shall
have been heard before any Judge having Jurisdiction in relation to such
Cause or Matter, and be then standing for Judgment, such Judge may at
any Time within Six Weeks after the Time when this Act comes into
operation give in to One of the Registrars attending the Court for Divorce
and Matrimonial Causes a written Judgment thereon signed by him; and a
Decree or Order, as the Case may require, shall be drawn up in pursuance
of such Judgment, and every such Decree or Order shall have the same
Force and Effect as if it had been drawn up in pursuance of a Judgment of
the Court for Divorce and Matrimonial Causes on the Day on which the
same was delivered to the Registrar, and shall be subject to Appeal under
this Act.

*Jurisdiction over Causes Matrimonial to be exercised by the Court for Divorce
and Matrimonial Causes.*

VI. As soon as this Act shall come into operation, all Jurisdiction now
vested in or exerciseable by any Ecclesiastical Court or Person in England in
respect of Divorces à Mensâ et Thoro, Suits of Nullity of Marriage, Suits
for Restitution of Conjugal Rights, or Jactitation of Marriage, and in all
Causes, Suits, and Matters Matrimonial, except in respect of Marriage
Licences, shall belong to and be vested in Her Majesty, and such Jurisdiction, together with the Jurisdiction conferred by this Act, shall be exercised
in the Name of Her Majesty in a Court of Record to be called "The Court
for Divorce and Matrimonial Causes."

*No Decree for Divorce à Mensâ et Thoro to be made hereafter, but a Judicial
Separation.*

VII. No Decree shall hereafter be made for a Divorce à Mensâ et Thoro,
but in all Cases in which a Decree for a Divorce à Mensâ et Thoro might now
be pronounced the Court may pronounce a Decree for a Judicial Separation,
which shall have the same Force and the same Consequences as a Divorce
à Mensâ et Thoro now has.

Judges of the Court.

VIII. The Lord Chancellor, the Lord Chief Justice of the Court of
Queen's Bench, the Lord Chief Justice of the Court of Common Pleas, the
Lord Chief Baron of the Court of Exchequer, the Senior Puisne Judge for
the Time being in each of the Three last-mentioned Courts, and the Judge
of Her Majesty's Court of Probate constituted by any Act of the present
Session, shall be the Judges of the said Court.

*Judge of the Court of Probate to be the Judge Ordinary, and shall have full
Authority, &c.*

IX. The Judge of the Court of Probate shall be called the Judge Ordinary
of the said Court, and shall have full Authority, either alone or with One or
more of the other Judges of the said Court, to hear and determine all
Matters arising therein, except Petitions for the dissolving of or annulling
Marriage, and Applications for new Trials of Questions or Issues before a
Jury, Bills of Exception, Special Verdicts, and Special Cases, and, except as
aforesaid, may exercise all the Powers and Authority of the said Court.

Petitions for Dissolution of a Marriage, &c. to be heard by Three Judges.

X. All Petitions, either for the Dissolution or for a Sentence of Nullity of
Marriage, and Applications for new Trials of Questions or Issues before a

Jury, shall be heard and determined by Three or more Judges of the said Court, of whom the Judge of the Court of Probate shall be One.

Who to act as Judge during Absence of the Judge Ordinary.

XI. During the temporary Absence of the Judge Ordinary, the Lord Chancellor may by Writing under his Hand authorize the Master of the Rolls, the Judge of the Admiralty Court, or either of the Lords Justices, or any Vice-Chancellor, or any Judge of the Superior Courts of Law at Westminster, to act as Judge Ordinary of the said Court for Divorce and Matrimonial Causes, and the Master of the Rolls, the Judge of the Admiralty Court, Lord Justice, Vice-Chancellor, or Judge of the Superior Courts, shall, when so acting, have and exercise all the Jurisdiction, Power, and Authority which might have been exercised by the Judge Ordinary.

Sittings of the Court.

XII. The Court for Divorce and Matrimonial Causes shall hold its Sittings at such Place or Places in London or Middlesex or elsewhere as Her Majesty in Council shall from Time to Time appoint.

Seal of the Court.

XIII. The Lord Chancellor shall direct a Seal to be made for the said Court, and may direct the same to be broken, altered, and renewed, at his Discretion; and all Decrees and Orders, or Copies of Decrees or Orders, of the said Court, sealed with the said Seal, shall be received in Evidence.

Officers of the Court.

XIV. The Registrars and other Officers of the Principal Registry of the Court of Probate shall attend the Sittings of the Court for Divorce and Matrimonial Causes, and assist in the Proceedings thereof, as shall be directed by the Rules and Orders under this Act.

Power to Advocates, Barristers, &c. of Ecclesiastical and Superior Courts to practise in the Court.

XV. All Persons admitted to practise as Advocates or Proctors respectively in any Ecclesiastical Court in England, and all Barristers, Attornies, and Solicitors entitled to practise in the Superior Courts at Westminster, shall be entitled to practise in the Court of Divorce and Matrimonial Causes; and such Advocates and Barristers shall have the same relative Rank and Precedence which they now have in the Judicial Committee of the Privy Council, unless and until Her Majesty shall otherwise order.

Sentence of Judicial Separation may be obtained by Husband or Wife for Adultery, &c.

XVI. A Sentence of Judicial Separation (which shall have the Effect of a Divorce à Mensâ et Thoro under the existing Law, and such other legal Effect as herein mentioned,) may be obtained, either by the Husband or the Wife, on the Ground of Adultery, or Cruelty, or Desertion without Cause for Two Years and upwards.

Application for Restitution of Conjugal Rights or Judicial Separation may be made by Husband or Wife by Petition to Court, &c.

XVII. Application for Restitution of Conjugal Rights or for Judicial Separation on any one of the Grounds aforesaid may be made by either Husband or Wife, by Petition to the Court, or to any Judge of Assize at the Assizes held for the County in which the Husband and Wife reside or last resided together, and which Judge of Assize is hereby authorized and required to hear and determine such Petition, according to the Rules and Regulations which shall be made under the Authority of this Act; and the Court or Judge to which such Petition is addressed, on being satisfied of the Truth of the Allegations therein contained, and that there is no legal Ground why the same should not be granted, may decree such Restitution of Conjugal Rights or Judicial Separation accordingly, and where the Application is by the Wife may make any Order for Alimony which shall be deemed just: Provided always, that any Judge of Assize to whom such Petition shall be presented may refer the same to any of Her Majesty's Counsel or Serjeant at Law named in the Commission of Assize or Nisi Prius, and such Counsel or Serjeant shall, for the Purpose of deciding upon the Matters of such Petition, have all the Powers that any such Judge would have had by virtue of this Act or otherwise.

Powers of Judges of Assize for Purposes of deciding Applications under Authority of this Act.

XVIII. For the Purpose of hearing and deciding all Applications under the Authority of this Act, the Judge of Assize or Person nominated by him as aforesaid shall be entitled to avail himself of the Services of all Officers, and use and exercise all Powers and Authorities, which the Court of Assize may employ, use, and exercise for the Determination of Causes and other Matters now usually heard and decided by them respectively, and the said Judge of Assize or other Person shall also for the Purpose have and be entitled to exercise all the Powers and Authorities hereby given to the Court for the hearing and deciding Applications made to it, and also the Powers hereby given to the Court to make Provision touching the Custody, Maintenance, and Education of Children; and every Order made by any Judge of Assize or other Person under the Authority of this Act may, on the Application of the Person obtaining the same, be entered as an Order of the Court, and when so entered shall have the same Force and Effect, and be enforced in the same Manner, as if such Order had been originally made by the Court.

The Court to regulate Fees on Proceedings before Judges, &c.

XIX. The Court shall from Time to Time fix and regulate the Fees which shall be payable upon all Proceedings under any Application to a Judge of Assize under this Act; and such Fees shall be received in Money, for their own Benefit, by the Persons to whom or for whose Use the same shall be directed to be paid.

Orders may be reviewed.

XX. Any Order so entered as aforesaid may be reviewed, and either altered or reversed on Appeal to the Judge Ordinary of the Court, but such Appeal shall not stay the intermediate Execution of the Order, unless the Judge Ordinary shall so direct, who shall have Power, if such Appeal be dismissed or abandoned, to order the Appellant to pay to the other Party the full Costs incurred by reason of such Appeal.

Wife deserted by her Husband may apply to a Police Magistrate or Justice in Petty Sessions for Protection.

XXI. A Wife deserted by her Husband may at any Time after such Desertion, if resident within the Metropolitan District, apply to a Police Magistrate, or if resident in the Country to Justices in Petty Sessions, or in either Case to the Court, for an Order to protect any Money or Property she may acquire by her own lawful Industry, and Property which she may become possessed of, after such Desertion, against her Husband or his Creditors, or any Person claiming under him; and such Magistrate or Justices or Court, if satisfied of the Fact of such Desertion, and that the same was without reasonable Cause, and that the Wife is maintaining herself by her own Industry or Property, may make and give to the Wife an Order protecting her Earnings and Property acquired since the Commencement of such Desertion from her Husband and all Creditors and Persons claiming under him, and such Earnings and Property shall belong to the Wife as if she were a Feme Sole: Provided always, that every such Order, if made by a Police Magistrate or Justices at Petty Sessions, shall, within Ten Days after the making thereof, be entered with the Registrar of the County Court within whose Jurisdiction the Wife is resident; and that it shall be lawful for the Husband, and any Creditor or other Person claiming under him, to apply to the Court, or to the Magistrate or Justices by whom such Order was made, for the Discharge thereof: Provided also, that if the Husband or any Creditor of or Person claiming under the Husband shall seize or continue to hold any Property of the Wife after Notice of any such Order, he shall be liable, at the Suit of the Wife (which she is hereby empowered to bring), to restore the specific Property, and also for a Sum equal to double the Value of the Property so seized or held after such Notice as aforesaid: If any such Order of Protection be made, the Wife shall during the Continuance thereof be and be deemed to have been, during such Desertion of her, in the like Position in all respects, with regard to Property and Contracts, and suing and being sued, as she would be under this Act if she obtained a Decree of Judicial Separation.

Court to act on Principles of the Ecclesiastical Courts.

XXII. In all Suits and Proceedings other than Proceedings to dissolve any Marriage the said Court shall proceed and act and give Relief on Principles and Rules which, in the Opinion of the said Court, shall be as nearly as may be conformable to the Principles and Rules on which the Ecclesiastical Courts have heretofore acted and given Relief, but subject to the Provisions herein contained and to the Rules and Orders under this Act.

Decree of Separation obtained during the Absence of Husband or Wife may be reversed.

XXIII. Any Husband or Wife, upon the Application of whose Wife or Husband, as the Case may be, a Decree of Judicial Separation has been pronounced, may, at any Time thereafter, present a Petition to the Court praying for a Reversal of such Decree on the Ground that it was obtained in his or her Absence, and that there was reasonable Ground for the alleged Desertion, where Desertion was the Ground of such Decree; and the Court may, on being satisfied of the Truth of the Allegations of such Petition, reverse the Decree accordingly, but the Reversal thereof shall not prejudice or affect the Rights or Remedies which any other Person would have had in case such Reversal had not been decreed, in respect of any Debts, Contracts, or Acts of the Wife incurred, entered into, or done between the Times of the Sentence of Separation and of the Reversal thereof.

Court may direct Payment of Alimony to Wife or to her Trustee.

XXIV. In all Cases in which the Court shall make any Decree or Order for Alimony, it may direct the same to be paid either to the Wife herself or to any Trustee on her Behalf, to be approved by the Court, and may impose any Terms or Restrictions which to the Court may seem expedient, and may from Time to Time appoint a new Trustee, if for any Reason it shall appear to the Court expedient so to do.

In case of Judicial Separation the Wife to be considered a Feme Sole with respect to Property she may acquire, &c.

XXV. In every Case of a Judicial Separation the Wife shall, from the Date of the Sentence and whilst the Separation shall continue, be considered as a Feme Sole with respect to Property of every Description which she may acquire or which may come to or devolve upon her; and such Property may be disposed of by her in all respects as a Feme Sole, and on her Decease the same shall, in case she shall die intestate, go as the same would have gone if her Husband had been then dead; provided, that if any such Wife should again cohabit with her Husband, all such Property as she may be entitled to when such Cohabitation shall take place shall be held to her separate Use, subject, however, to any Agreement in Writing made between herself and her Husband whilst separate.

Also for Purposes of Contract and suing.

XXVI. In every Case of a Judicial Separation the Wife shall, whilst so separated, be considered as a Feme Sole for the Purposes of Contract, and Wrongs and Injuries, and suing and being sued in any Civil Proceeding; and her Husband shall not be liable in respect of any Engagement or Contract she may have entered into, or for any wrongful Act or Omission by her, or for any Costs she may incur as Plaintiff or Defendant; provided, that where upon any such Judicial Separation Alimony has been decreed or ordered to be paid to the Wife, and the same shall not be duly paid by the Husband, he shall be liable for Necessaries supplied for her Use; provided also, that nothing shall prevent the Wife from joining, at any Time during such Separation, in the Exercise of any joint Power given to herself and her Husband.

On Adultery of Wife or Incest, &c. of Husband, Petition for Dissolution of Marriage may be presented. As to "Incestuous Adultery."

XXVII. It shall be lawful for any Husband to present a Petition to the said Court, praying that his Marriage may be dissolved, on the Ground that his Wife has since the Celebration thereof been guilty of Adultery; and it shall be lawful for any Wife to present a Petition to the said Court, praying that her Marriage may be dissolved, on the Ground that since the Celebration thereof her Husband has been guilty of incestuous Adultery, or of Bigamy with Adultery, or of Rape, or of Sodomy or Bestiality, or of Adultery coupled with such Cruelty as without Adultery would have entitled her to a Divorce à Mensâ et Thoro, or of Adultery coupled with Desertion, without reasonable Excuse, for Two Years or upwards; and every such Petition shall state as distinctly as the Nature of the Case permits the Facts on which the Claim to have such Marriage dissolved is founded: Provided that for the Purposes of this Act incestuous Adultery shall be taken to mean Adultery committed by a Husband with a Woman with whom if his Wife were dead he could not lawfully contract Marriage by reason of her being within the prohibited Degrees of Consanguinity or Affinity; and Bigamy shall be taken to mean Marriage of any Person, being married, to any other Person during the Life of the former Husband or Wife, whether the Second

Marriage shall have taken place within the Dominions of Her Majesty or elsewhere.

Adulterer to be a Co-Respondent.   Case may be tried by a Jury.

XXVIII. Upon any such Petition presented by a Husband the Petitioner shall make the alleged Adulterer a Co-Respondent to the said Petition, unless on special Grounds, to be allowed by the Court, he shall be excused from so doing; and on every Petition presented by a Wife for Dissolution of Marriage the Court, if it see fit, may direct that the Person with whom the Husband is alleged to have committed Adultery be made a Respondent; and the Parties or either of them may insist on having the contested Matters of Fact tried by a Jury as herein-after mentioned.

Court to be satisfied of Absence of Collusion.

XXIX. Upon any such Petition for the Dissolution of a Marriage, it shall be the Duty of the Court to satisfy itself, so far as it reasonably can, not only as to the Facts alleged, but also whether or no the Petitioner has been in any Manner accessory to or conniving at the Adultery, or has condoned the same, and shall also inquire into any Counter-charge which may be made against the Petitioner.

Dismissal of Petition.

XXX. In case the Court, on the Evidence in relation to any such Petition, shall not be satisfied that the alleged Adultery has been committed, or shall find that the Petitioner has during the Marriage been accessory to or conniving at the Adultery of the other Party to the Marriage, or has condoned the Adultery complained of, or that the Petition is presented or prosecuted in collusion with either of the Respondents, then and in any of the said Cases the Court shall dismiss the said Petition.

Power to Court to pronounce Decree for dissolving Marriage.

XXXI. In case the Court shall be satisfied on the Evidence that the Case of the Petitioner has been proved, and shall not find that the Petitioner has been in any Manner accessory to or conniving at the Adultery of the other Party to the Marriage, or has condoned the Adultery complained of, or that the Petition is presented or prosecuted in collusion with either of the Respondents, then the Court shall pronounce a Decree declaring such Marriage to be dissolved : Provided always, that the Court shall not be bound to pronounce such Decree if it shall find that the Petitioner has during the Marriage been guilty of Adultery, or if the Petitioner shall, in the Opinion of the Court, have been guilty of unreasonable Delay in presenting or prosecuting such Petition, or of Cruelty towards the other Party to the Marriage, or of having deserted or wilfully separated himself or herself from the other Party before the Adultery complained of, and without reasonable Excuse, or of such wilful Neglect or Misconduct as has conduced to the Adultery.

Alimony.

XXXII. The Court may, if it shall think fit, on any such Decree, order that the Husband shall to the Satisfaction of the Court secure to the Wife such gross Sum of Money, or such annual Sum of Money for any Term not exceeding her own Life, as, having regard to her Fortune (if any), to the Ability of the Husband, and to the Conduct of the Parties, it shall deem reasonable, and for that Purpose may refer it to any one of the Conveyancing Counsel of the Court of Chancery to settle and approve of a proper Deed or Instrument to be executed by all necessary Parties; and the said Court may in such Case, if it shall see fit, suspend the pronouncing of its Decree until such Deed shall have been duly executed; and upon any Petition for Dissolution of Marriage the Court shall have the same Power to make interim Orders for Payment of Money, by way of Alimony or otherwise, to the Wife, as it would have in a Suit instituted for Judicial Separation.

Husband may claim Damages from Adulterers.

XXXIII. Any Husband may, either in a Petition for Dissolution of Marriage or for Judicial Separation, or in a Petition limited to such Object only, claim Damages from any Person on the Ground of his having committed Adultery with the Wife of such Petitioner, and such Petition shall be served on the alleged Adulterer and the Wife, unless the Court shall dispense with such Service, or direct some other Service to be substituted; and the Claim made by every such Petition shall be heard and tried on the same Principles, in the same Manner, and subject to the same or the like Rules and Regulations as Actions for Criminal Conversation are now tried and decided in Courts of Common Law; and all the Enactments herein contained with reference to the Hearing and Decision of Petitions to the Court shall, so far as may be necessary, be deemed applicable to the Hearing and Decision of Petitions presented under this Enactment; and the Damages to be recovered on any such Petition shall in all Cases be ascertained by the Verdict of a Jury, although the Respondents or either of them may not appear; and after the Verdict has been given the Court shall have Power to direct in what Manner such Damages shall be paid or applied, and to direct that the whole or any Part thereof shall be settled for the Benefit of the Children (if any) of the Marriage, or as a Provision for the Maintenance of the Wife.

Power to Court to order Adulterer to pay Costs.

XXXIV. Whenever in any Petition presented by a Husband the alleged Adulterer shall have been made a Co-Respondent, and the Adultery shall have been established, it shall be lawful for the Court to order the Adulterer to pay the whole or any Part of the Costs of the Proceedings.

Power to Court to make Orders as to Custody of Children.

XXXV. In any Suit or other Proceeding for obtaining a Judicial Separation or a Decree of Nullity of Marriage, and on any Petition for dissolving a Marriage, the Court may from Time to Time, before making its final Decree, make such interim Orders, and may make such Provision in the final Decree, as it may deem just and proper with respect to the Custody, Maintenance, and Education of the Children the Marriage of whose Parents is the Subject of such Suit or other Proceeding, and may, if it shall think fit, direct proper Proceedings to be taken for placing such Children under the Protection of the Court of Chancery.

Questions of Fact may be tried before the Court.

XXXVI. In Questions of Fact arising in Proceedings under this Act it shall be lawful for, but, except as herein-before provided, not obligatory upon, the Court to direct the Truth thereof to be determined before itself, or before any One or more of the Judges of the said Court, by the Verdict of a Special or Common Jury.

Where a Question is ordered to be tried a Jury may be summoned as in the Common Law Courts. Rights to Challenge.

XXXVII. The Court, or any Judge thereof, may make all such Rules and Orders upon the Sheriff or any other Person for procuring the Attendance of a Special or Common Jury for the Trial of such Question as may now be made by any of the Superior Courts of Common Law at Westminster, and may also make any other Orders which to such Court or Judge may seem requisite ; and every such Jury shall consist of Persons possessing the like Qualifications, and shall be struck, summoned, balloted for, and called in like Manner, as if such Jury were a Jury for the Trial of any Cause in any of the said Superior Courts; and every Juryman so summoned shall be entitled to the same Rights, and subject to the same Duties and Liabilities, as if he had been duly summoned for the Trial of any such Cause in any of the said Superior Courts ; and every Party to any such Proceeding shall be entitled to the same Rights as to Challenge and otherwise as if he were a Party to any such Cause.

Such Question to be reduced into Writing and a Jury to be sworn to try it. Judge to have same Powers as at Nisi Prius.

XXXVIII. When any such Question shall be so ordered to be tried such Question shall be reduced into Writing in such Form as the Court shall direct, and at the Trial the Jury shall be sworn to try the said Question, and a true Verdict to give thereon according to the Evidence; and upon every such Trial the Court or Judge shall have the same Powers, Jurisdiction, and Authority as any Judge of any of the said Superior Courts sitting at Nisi Prius.

Bill of Exceptions, Special Verdict, and Special Case.

XXXIX. Upon the Trial of any such Question or of any Issue under this Act a Bill of Exceptions may be tendered, and a General or Special Verdict or Verdicts, subject to a Special Case, may be returned, in like Manner as in any Cause tried in any of the said Superior Courts; and every such Bill of Exceptions, Special Verdict, and Special Case respectively shall be stated, settled, and sealed in like Manner as in any Cause tried in any of the said Superior Courts, and where the Trial shall not have been had in the Court for Divorce and Matrimonial Causes shall be returned into such Court without any Writ of Error or other Writ; and the Matter of Law in every such Bill of Exceptions, Special Verdict, and Special Case shall be heard and determined by the full Courts, subject to such Right of Appeal as is hereinafter given in other Cases.

Court may direct Issues to try any Fact.

XL. It shall be lawful for the Court to direct One or more Issue or Issues to be tried in any Court of Common Law, and either before a Judge of Assize in any County or at the Sittings for the Trial of Causes in London or Middlesex, and either by a Special or Common Jury, in like Manner as is now done by the Court of Chancery.

Affidavit in support of a Petition.

XLI. Every Person seeking a Decree of Nullity of Marriage, or a Decree of Judicial Separation, or a Dissolution of Marriage, or Decree in a Suit of Jactitation of Marriage, shall, together with the Petition or other Application for the same, file an Affidavit verifying the same, so far as he or she is able to do so, and stating that there is not any Collusion or Connivance between the Deponent and the other Party to the Marriage.

Service of Petition.

XLII. Every such Petition shall be served on the Party to .be affected thereby, either within or without Her Majesty's Dominions, in such Manner as the Court shall by any General or Special Order from Time to Time direct, and for that Purpose the Court shall have all the Powers conferred by any Statute on the Court of Chancery : Provided always, that the said Court may dispense with such Service altogether in case it shall seem necessary or expedient so to do.

Examination of Petitioner.

XLIII. The Court may, if it shall think fit, order the Attendance of the Petitioner, and may examine him or her, or permit him or her to be examined or cross-examined on Oath on the Hearing of any Petition, but no such Petitioner shall be bound to answer any Question tending to show that he or she has been guilty of Adultery.

Adjournment.

XLIV. The Court may from Time to Time adjourn the Hearing of any such Petition, and may require further Evidence thereon, if it shall see fit so to do.

Court may order Settlement of Property for Benefit of innocent Party and Children of Marriage.

XLV. In any Case in which the Court shall pronounce a Sentence of Divorce or Judicial Separation for Adultery of the Wife, if it shall be made appear to the Court that the Wife is entitled to any Property either in possession or reversion, it shall be lawful for the Court, if it shall think proper, to order such Settlement as it shall think reasonable to be made of such Property or any Part thereof, for the Benefit of the innocent Party, and of the Children of the Marriage, or either or any of them.

Mode of taking Evidence.

XLVI. Subject to such Rules and Regulations as may be established as herein provided, the Witnesses in all Proceedings before the Court where their Attendance can be had shall be sworn and examined orally in open Court : Provided that Parties, except as herein-before provided, shall be at liberty to verify their respective Cases in whole or in part by Affidavit, but so that the Deponent in every such Affidavit shall, on the Application of the opposite Party, or by Direction of the Court, be subject to be cross-examined by or on behalf of the opposite Party orally in open Court, and after such Cross-examination may be re-examined orally in open Court as aforesaid by or on behalf of the Party by whom such Affidavit was filed.

Court may issue Commissions or give Orders for Examination of Witnesses abroad, or unable to attend.

XLVII. Provided, That where a Witness is out of the Jurisdiction of the Court, or where, by reason of his Illness or from other Circumstances, the Court shall not think fit to enforce the Attendance of the Witness in open Court, it shall be lawful for the Court to order a Commission to issue for the Examination of such Witness on Oath, upon Interrogatories or other-

wise, or if the Witness be within the Jurisdiction of the Court to order the
Examination of such Witness on Oath, upon Interrogatories or otherwise,
before any Officer of the said Court, or other Person to be named in such
Order for the Purpose; and all the Powers given to the Courts of Law at
Westminster by the Acts of the Thirteenth Year of King George the Third,
Chapter Sixty-three, and of the First Year of King William the Fourth,
Chapter Twenty-two, for enabling the Courts of Law at Westminster to issue
Commissions and give Orders for the Examination of Witnesses in Actions
depending in such Courts, and to enforce such Examination, and all the
Provisions of the said Acts, and of any other Acts for enforcing or otherwise
applicable to such Examination and the Witnesses examined, shall extend
and be applicable to the Court and to the Examination of Witnesses under
the Commissions and Orders of the said Court, and to the Witnesses
examined, as if such Court were One of the Courts of Law at Westminster,
and the Matter before it were an Action pending in such Court.

Rules of Evidence in Common Law Courts to be observed.

XLVIII. The Rules of Evidence observed in the Superior Courts of
Common Law at Westminster shall be applicable to and observed in the
Trial of all Questions of Fact in the Court.

Attendance of Witnesses on the Court.

XLIX. The Court may, under its Seal, issue Writs of Subpœna or Subpœna duces tecum, commanding the Attendance of Witnesses at such Time
and Place as shall be therein expressed; and such Writs may be served in
any Part of Great Britain or Ireland; and every Person served with such
Writ shall be bound to attend, and to be sworn and give Evidence in obedience thereto, in the same Manner as if it had been a Writ of Subpœna
or Subpœna duces tecum issued from any of the said Superior Courts of
Common Law in a Cause pending therein, and served in Great Britain or
Ireland, as the Case may be: Provided that any Petitioner required to be
examined, or any Person called as a Witness or required or desiring to make
an Affidavit or Deposition under or for the Purposes of this Act, shall be
permitted to make his solemn Affirmation or Declaration instead of being
sworn in the Circumstances and Manner in which a Person called as a Witness or desiring to make an Affidavit or Deposition would be permitted so to
do under the "Common Law Procedure Act, 1854," in Cases within the
Provisions of that Act.

Penalties for false Evidence.

L. All Persons wilfully deposing or affirming falsely in any Proceeding
before the Court shall be deemed to be guilty of Perjury, and shall be liable
to all the Pains and Penalties attached thereto.

Costs.

LI. The Court on the Hearing of any Suit, Proceeding, or Petition under
this Act, and the House of Lords on the Hearing of any Appeal under this
Act, may make such Order as to Costs as to such Court or House respectively may seem just: Provided always, that there shall be no Appeal on the
Subject of Costs only.

Enforcement of Orders and Decrees.

LII. All Decrees and Orders to be made by the Court in any Suit, Proceeding, or Petition to be instituted under Authority of this Act shall

be enforced and put in execution in the same or the like Manner as the Judgments, Orders, and Decrees of the High Court of Chancery may be now enforced and put in execution.

Power to make Rules, &c. for Procedure, and to alter them from Time to Time.

LIII. The Court shall make such Rules and Regulations concerning the Practice and Procedure under this Act as it may from Time to Time consider expedient, and shall have full Power from Time to Time to revoke or alter the same.

Fees to be regulated.

LIV. The Court shall have full Power to fix and regulate from Time to Time the Fees payable upon all Proceedings before it, all which Fees shall be received, paid, and applied as herein directed: Provided always, that the said Court may make such Rules and Regulations as it may deem necessary and expedient for enabling Persons to sue in the said Court in formâ pauperis.

Appeal from the Judge Ordinary to the full Court.

LV. Either Party dissatisfied with any Decision of the Court in any Matter which, according to the Provisions aforesaid, may be made by the Judge Ordinary alone, may, within Three Calendar Months after the pronouncing thereof, appeal therefrom to the full Court, whose Decision shall be final.

Appeal to the House of Lords in case of Petition for Dissolution of a Marriage.

LVI. Either Party dissatisfied with the Decision of the full Court on any Petition for the Dissolution of a Marriage may, within Three Months after the pronouncing thereof, appeal therefrom to the House of Lords if Parliament be then sitting, or if Parliament be not sitting at the End of such Three Months, then within Fourteen Days next after its meeting; and on the Hearing of any such Appeal the House of Lords may either dismiss the Appeal or reverse the Decree, or remit the Case to the Court, to be dealt with in all respects as the House of Lords shall direct.

Liberty to Parties to marry again. No Clergyman compelled to solemnize certain Marriages.

LVII. When the Time hereby limited for appealing against any Decree dissolving a Marriage shall have expired, and no Appeal shall have been presented against such Decree, or when any such Appeal shall have been dismissed, or when in the Result of any Appeal any Marriage shall be declared to be dissolved, but not sooner, it shall be lawful for the respective Parties thereto to marry again, as if the prior Marriage had been dissolved by Death: Provided always, that no Clergyman in Holy Orders of the United Church of England and Ireland shall be compelled to solemnize the Marriage of any Person whose former Marriage may have been dissolved on the Ground of his or her Adultery, or shall be liable to any Suit, Penalty, or Censure for solemnizing or refusing to solemnize the Marriage of any such Person.

If Minister of any Church, &c. refuses to perform Marriage Ceremony, any other Minister may perform such Service.

LVIII. Provided always, that when any Minister of any Church or Chapel of the United Church of England and Ireland shall refuse to perform such Marriage Service between any Persons who but for such Refusal would be entitled to have the same Service performed in such Church or Chapel, such Minister shall permit any other Minister in Holy Orders of the said United Church, entitled to officiate within the Diocese in which such Church or Chapel is situate, to perform such Marriage Service in such Church or Chapel.

No Action in England for Criminal Conversation.

LIX. After this Act shall have come into operation no Action shall be maintainable in England for Criminal Conversation.

All Fees, except as herein provided, to be collected by Stamps.

LX. None of the Fees payable under this Act, except as herein expressly provided, shall be received in Money, but every such Fee shall be collected and received by a Stamp denoting the Amount of the Fee which would otherwise be payable; and the Fees to be so collected by Stamps shall be " Stamp Duties," and be under the Management of the Commissioners of Inland Revenue.

Provisions concerning Stamps for the Court of Probate to be applicable to the Purposes of this Act.

LXI. The Provisions contained in or referred to by an Act of the present Session of Parliament, " to amend the Laws relating to Probates and Letters of Administration in England," and applicable to the Collection and Payment and Accounts of the Fees to be received thereunder by means of Stamps, and to such Stamps, and the Vellum, Parchment, or Paper on or to which the same shall be impressed or affixed, and in relation to Documents which ought to have Stamps impressed thereon or affixed thereto, and to the Punishment of Persons for such wrongful Acts as therein mentioned in relation to Stamps, or Fees or Sums of Money which ought to be collected by means of Stamps, shall be applicable to and for the Purposes of this Act, as if such Provisions as aforesaid had been contained or referred to in this Act with reference to the like Matters, and the Court under this Act had been mentioned, instead of the Court of Probate, or the Judge thereof, as the Case may be.

Expenses of the Court to be paid out of Monies to be provided by Parliament.

LXII. It shall be lawful for the Commissioners of Her Majesty's Treasury, out of such Monies as may be provided and appropriated by Parliament for the Purpose, to cause to be paid all necessary Expenses of the Court under this Act, and other Expenses which may be incurred in carrying the Provisions of this Act into effect, except as herein otherwise provided.

Stamp Duty on Admission of Proctors and annual Certificates.

LXIII. The same Amount of Stamp Duty as is now payable on the Admission of a Proctor to any Ecclesiastical Court shall be payable by every Person to be admitted as a Proctor in the Court of Divorce and Matrimonial Causes, or in the Court of Probate, who shall not have been previously admitted as a Proctor in the other of such Courts, or in an Ecclesiastical or Admiralty Court, and have paid the Stamp Duty in respect thereof; and every Person who shall practise as a Proctor or as a Solicitor or Attorney in the said Court of Divorce and Matrimonial Causes, or the said Court of Probate, shall obtain an annual Certificate to authorize him so to do, under

the Stamp Duty Acts, in the same Manner as Proctors practising in the
Ecclesiastical or Admiralty Courts, and Solicitors and Attornies practising
in Her Majesty's Courts at Westminster, are now required to do by the
said Acts or any of them, and shall be subject and liable to the same
Penalties and Disabilities in case of any Neglect to obtain such Certificates
as such Proctors, Attornies, and Solicitors are now subject and liable to for
any similar Neglect, and as if the Clauses and Provisions of the said Acts
in relation to such Certificates had been inserted in this Act, and specially
enacted in reference to Proctors, Solicitors, and Attornies practising in the
said Court of Divorce and Matrimonial Causes and Court of Probate, provided that One annual Certificate only shall be required for any one Person, although he may practise in more than One of the Capacities aforesaid,
or in several of the Courts herein-before mentioned.

Compensation to Proctors.

LXIV. Every Person who at the Time of the passing of this Act has been
duly admitted and is practising as a Proctor in any Ecclesiastical Court in
England shall, at the Expiration of Two Years from and after the Commencement of this Act, be entitled to make a Claim for Compensation to
the Commissioners of Her Majesty's Treasury; and the said Commissioners,
by Examination of Evidence on Oath (which they are hereby empowered to
administer), or otherwise, as they shall think fit, shall inquire into and
ascertain the Loss, if any, of Professional Gains and Profits in respect of
Suits relating to Marriage and Divorce sustained by such Proctors respectively, upon a Comparison in each Case of the average clear Gains of the
Three Years immediately before the Commencement of this Act, arising
from such last-mentioned Business, and the Average of the same Gains
during the Two Years immediately succeeding the Commencement of this
Act; and the said Commissioners shall in each Case, having regard to all
the Circumstances, award a reasonable Compensation, by way of Annuity, to
the Persons sustaining such Loss, during their Lives, but in no Case shall
such Annuity exceed One Half of the annual Loss so ascertained as aforesaid; and such Annuities shall be paid out of Monies to be annually provided by Parliament for that Purpose, and the Persons receiving the same
shall be subject to the Provisions contained in the Nineteenth Section of the
Act of Fourth and Fifth William the Fourth, Chapter Twenty-four.

As to Salary of Judge of Court of Probate, if appointed Judge of Court of Divorce, &c.

LXV. In case the Judge of the Court of Probate established by any Act
passed during the present Session shall be appointed Judge Ordinary of the
Court for Divorce and Matrimonial Causes, the Salary of such Judge shall
be the Sum of Five thousand Pounds per Annum; but such Judge, if afterwards appointed Judge of the Admiralty Court, shall not be entitled to any
Increase of Salary.

Power to Secretary of State to order all Letters Patent, Records, &c. to be trans-mitted from all Ecclesiastical Courts. Penalty on disobeying such Order.

LXVI. Any One of Her Majesty's Principal Secretaries of State may
order every Judge, Registrar, or other Officer of any Ecclesiastical Court in
England or the Isle of Man, or any other Person having the public Custody
of or Control over any Letters Patent, Records, Deeds, Processes, Acts,

Proceedings, Books, Documents, or other Instrument relating to Marriages, or to Suits for Divorce, Nullity of Marriage, Restitution of Conjugal Rights, or to any other Matters or Causes Matrimonial, except Marriage Licences, to transmit the same, at such Times and in such Manner, to such Places in London or Westminster, and under such Regulations, as the said Secretary of State may appoint; and if any Judge, Registrar, Officer, or other Person shall wilfully disobey such Order, he shall for the First Offence forfeit the Sum of One hundred Pounds, to be recoverable by any Registrar of the Court of Probate as a Debt under this Act in any of the Superior Courts at Westminster, and for the Second and subsequent Offences the Judge Ordinary may commit the Person so offending to Prison for any Period not exceeding Three Calendar Months, provided that the Warrant of Committal be countersigned by One of Her Majesty's Principal Secretaries of State, and the said Persons so offending shall forfeit all Claim to Compensation under this Act.

Rules, &c. to be laid before Parliament.

LXVII. All Rules and Regulations concerning Practice or Procedure, or fixing or regulating Fees, which may be made by the Court under this Act, shall be laid before both Houses of Parliament within One Month after the making thereof, if Parliament be then sitting, or if Parliament be not then sitting, within One Month after the Commencement of the then next Session of Parliament.

Yearly Account of Fees, &c. to be laid before Parliament.

LXVIII. The Judge Ordinary of the Court for Divorce and Matrimonial Causes for the Time being shall cause to be prepared in each Year ending December Thirty-one a Return of all Fees and Monies levied in such Year on account of the Fee Fund of the Court of Divorce and Matrimonial Causes, and of any other Fund under the Authority of this Act; also, a Return of the annual Salaries of the said Judge Ordinary, and of all Persons holding Offices in the said Court, with all the incidental Expenses of the said Court, whether the Salaries and incidental Expenses aforesaid be defrayed out of Fees or out of any other Monies; also, a Return of all Superannuations, Pensions, Annuities, retiring Allowances, and Compensations made payable under this Act, in each Year, stating the gross Amount, and the Amount in detail, of such Charges: Provided always, that all such Returns as aforesaid shall be presented to both Houses of Parliament on or before the Thirty-first Day of March in each Year, if Parliament is then sitting, and if Parliament is not sitting, then such Returns shall be presented within One Month of the First Meeting of Parliament after the Thirty-first Day of March in each Year.

RULES AND ORDERS

HER MAJESTY'S COURT FOR DIVORCE AND MATRIMONIAL CAUSES,

*Made under the Provisions of the "Act to amend the Law relating to Divorce
"and Matrimonial Causes in England"* (20 & 21 Vict. Cap. 85).

---

1. PROCEEDINGS before the Court for Divorce and Matrimonial Causes shall be commenced by filing a petition. A Form of such Petition is given, No. 3.

2. Every such petition shall be accompanied by an affidavit made by the Petitioner, verifying the facts stated in the petition of which he or she has personal cognizance, and such affidavit shall be filed with the petition.

3. In cases where the Petitioner is seeking a decree of nullity of marriage, or a decree of judicial separation, or a dissolution of marriage, or a decree in a suit of jactitation of marriage, the Petitioner's affidavit, filed with his or her petition, shall further state that no collusion or connivance exists between the Petitioner and the other party to the marriage or alleged marriage.

4. Every petitioner who files a petition and affidavit shall forthwith issue a citation, to be served on the Respondent in the cause, according to the Form No. 1.

5. A similar citation shall be served upon any party whom it is intended to make a Co-respondent in the cause.

6. To each Respondent in the cause shall be delivered, together with the citation, a copy of the petition certified under the seal of the Court.

7. Every citation shall be written or printed on parchment, and the party taking out the same, or his or her proctor, solicitor, or attorney, shall take it, together with a præcipe, to the Registry, and there deposit the præcipe and get the citation signed and sealed.—The Form of Præcipe is given, No. 2.

8. The party applying for a citation to be sealed shall, on depositing the præcipe in the Registry, give an address within three miles of the General Post Office, at which it shall be sufficient to leave all notices, instruments, and other proceedings not by these Rules and Orders expressly requiring personal service.

9. Before a party can proceed after the service of a citation, unless by the express leave of the Court, an appearance must have been previously entered by or on the behalf of the party cited, or an affidavit of personal service of the citation must have been filed in the Registry.

M

10. In cases where personal service cannot be effected, application may be made to the Judge Ordinary, upon motion in open court, to substitute some other mode of service, or to dispense with service altogether.

11. Personal service of a citation shall be effected by leaving a copy of the citation with the party cited, and producing the original, if required by him or her so to do.

12. Every entry of an appearance shall be accompanied by an address within three miles of the General Post Office, at which it shall be sufficient to leave all notices, instruments, and other proceedings.

13. After personal service of citation has been effected, the citation, with the certificate of service endorsed thereon, shall be forthwith returned into and filed in the Registry.

14. Within twenty-one days from the service of the citation the Respondent shall file his or her answer in the Registry, otherwise the Petitioner shall be at liberty to proceed to proof of the petition.—A Form of Answer is given, No. 4.

15. Every answer which contains matter other than a simple denial of the facts stated in the petition, shall be accompanied by an affidavit made by the Respondent, verifying such other or additional matter, and such affidavit shall be filed with the answer.

16. In cases involving a decree of nullity of marriage, or a decree of judicial separation, or a dissolution of marriage, or a decree in a suit of jactitation of marriage, the Respondent shall, in the affidavit filed with the answer, further state that there is not any collusion or connivance between the Deponent and the other party to the marriage.

17. The Respondent shall file his or her answer in the Registry, and on the same day deliver to the Petitioner, or his or her proctor, solicitor, or attorney, a copy thereof.

18. Within fifteen days from the filing of the answer the Petitioner may file a reply thereto, and the same period shall be allowed for bringing in and filing any further statement by way of answer to such replication.

19. If either party desire to amend his or her petition, answer, or subsequent statement, it may be done by permission of the Judge Ordinary, and in such form and under such terms as the Judge Ordinary may approve.

20. When the proceedings have raised the questions of fact necessary to be determined, either party may, within fifteen days from the filing of the last proceeding, apply to the Judge Ordinary to direct the truth of any question of fact arising in the proceedings to be tried by a jury.

21. If neither party claim that the cause shall be heard before a jury, the Judge Ordinary shall determine whether the same shall be tried by a jury, or before the Court itself, and whether by oral evidence or upon affidavit.

22. Whenever a case is to be tried before a jury, the Judge Ordinary shall direct the questions at issue to be stated in the form of a record, to be settled by one of the Registrars.—A Form of Record is given, No. 11.

23. After the record has been so settled, either party shall be at liberty to apply to the Judge Ordinary to alter or amend the same, and his decision shall be final, and binding on the parties.

24. The Petitioner shall file the record and set down the cause as ready for trial, and on the day upon which it is set down shall give notice of his or her having done so to each party for whom an appearance has been entered; and if the Petitioner delay filing the record and setting down the cause as ready for trial, for the space of one month from the day on which the record was finally settled, the Respondent may file the record and set the cause down as ready for trial, and give a similar notice to the Petitioner and the aforesaid other parties. A copy of every such notice shall be filed in the Registry, and the cause, unless the Judge Ordinary shall otherwise direct, shall come on in its turn.

25. When an affidavit establishing the factum of a marriage between the parties has been filed, and the husband has appeared in the cause, the wife mar proceed to file a petition for alimony, in substance according to the Form No. 12; and a copy of such petition shall be served on the husband, or on his proctor, solicitor, or attorney, on the same day.

26. The husband shall, within eight days after a petition for alimony has been filed, file his answer thereto upon oath, and on the same day deliver a copy thereof to the wife, or to her proctor, solicitor, or attorney.

27. The wife, subject to any order as to costs, may, if not satisfied with the husband's answer, examine witnesses in support of her petition for alimony.

28. After the answer of the husband has been filed, the wife may, at its next sitting, move the Court to decree her alimony *pendente lite;* provided that the wife shall, two days at least before she so moves the Court, give notice to her husband, or to his proctor, solicitor, or attorney, of her intention so to do.

29. A wife who has obtained a decree of judicial separation in her favour, and has previously filed her petition for alimony, may, unless in cases where an appeal to the full Court is interposed, move the Court to decree her permanent alimony; provided that she shall, eight days at least before making any such motion, give notice to the husband, or to his proctor, solicitor, or attorney, of her intention so to do.

30. Where a decree of judicial separation has been pronounced, it shall not be necessary for either party to enter into a bond conditioned against marrying again.

31. Every subpœna shall be written or printed on parchment, and may include the names of any number of witnesses. The party issuing the same, or his or her proctor, solicitor, or attorney, shall take it, together with a præcipe, to the Registry, and there get it signed and sealed, and there deposit the præcipe.—Forms of Subpœna are given, Nos. 6 and 8; and Forms of Præcipe, Nos. 7 and 9.

32. The Petitioner or Respondent may call upon the other party, by notice in writing, to admit any document, saving any just exceptions; and in case of refusal or neglect to admit the same, the costs of proving the docu-

ment shall be paid by the parties so neglecting or refusing, whatever the
result of the cause may be, unless the Judge Ordinary shall certify that the
refusal to admit was reasonable; and when such notice to admit has not been
given, no costs of proving any document shall be given, except in cases where
the omission to give the notice is in the opinion of the Registrar a saving of
expense.

33. The hearing of the cause shall be conducted in court, and the counsel
shall address the Court, subject to the same rules and regulations as now
obtain in the Courts of Common Law.

34. The Registrar shall, in cases tried by a jury, enter on the record the
finding of the jury and the decree of the Court, and shall sign the same. In
all cases the Registrar shall enter the decree of the Court in the Court
Book.

35. In cases to be tried upon affidavit the Petitioner and Respondent shall
file the affidavits within eight days from the filing of the last proceeding.

36. Counter-affidavits to any facts stated in any such affidavits may be filed
by either party within fifteen days from the filing of the affidavit which they
are intended to answer.

37. Affidavits in reply to counter-affidavits may be filed by permission of
the Judge Ordinary, granted on motion or summons, but not otherwise.

38. Applications to produce a Deponent in the cause, for the purpose of
cross-examination, shall be made on summons to the Judge Ordinary sitting
in Chambers.

39. Applications on the part of a wife deserted by her husband for an
order to protect her earnings and property, acquired since the commencement of such desertion, shall be made on summons to the Judge Ordinary
in Chambers, and supported by affidavit.—A Form of Application is given,
No. 13.

40. Applications for the discharge of any Order made to protect the
earnings and property of the wife are to be founded on affidavit.

41. Petitions to the Court for the reversal of a decree of judicial separation must set out the grounds upon which the Petitioner relies, as in Form
No. 14.

42. Any person desirous of prosecuting a suit *in formâ pauperis* shall lay
a case before counsel, and obtain an opinion from such counsel that he or
she has reasonable grounds for applying to the Court for relief.

43. No person shall be admitted to prosecute a suit *in formâ pauperis*
without the order of the Judge Ordinary; and to obtain such order the case
laid before counsel for his opinion, and his opinion thereon, with an affidavit
of the party or of his or her attorney that the same case contains a full
and true statement of all the material facts, to the best of his or her
knowledge and belief, and an affidavit by the party applying that he or she is
not worth 25*l.*, after payment of his or her just debts, save and except
his or her wearing apparel, shall be produced at the time such application is
made.

44. Where a pauper omits to proceed to trial pursuant to notice, he or she may be called upon by summons to show cause why he or she should not pay costs, though he or she has not been dispaupered, and why all further proceedings should not be stayed until such costs be paid.

45. Every application for a new trial in respect of causes tried before a jury is to be lodged in the Registry within a month from the day on which the cause was tried.

46. If the Petitioner or Respondent, unless by leave of the Judge Ordinary previously obtained, fail to deliver the answer, reply, or other proceeding within the time specified in these Rules, the other party shall not be compelled to receive the same, unless by direction of the Judge Ordinary. The expense of every such application to the Judge Ordinary shall fall on the party causing the delay, unless the Judge Ordinary shall otherwise direct.

47. Where a special time is limited for filing affidavits, no affidavit filed after that time shall be used unless by leave of the Judge Ordinary.

48. Wherever it becomes necessary to give a notice to the opposite party in the cause, such notice shall be in writing, signed by the party, or by his or her proctor, solicitor, or attorney.

49. The addition and true place of abode of every person making an affidavit is to be inserted therein.

50. In every affidavit made by two or more persons the names of the several persons making it are to be written in the jurat.

51. No affidavit shall be read or made use of in any matter depending in court in the jurat of which there is any interlineation or erasure.

52. Where an affidavit is made by any person who is blind, or who, from his or her signature or otherwise, appears to be illiterate, the person before whom such affidavit is made is to state in the jurat that the affidavit was read in the presence of the party making the same, and that such party seemed to, and according to the belief of such person did, understand the same, and also that the said party made his or her mark or wrote his or her signature in the presence of the person before whom the affidavit was made.

53. No affidavit is to be deemed sufficient which has been sworn before the party on whose behalf the same is offered, or before his or her proctor, solicitor, or attorney, or before a clerk of his proctor, solicitor, or attorney.

54. A proctor, solicitor, or attorney, and their clerks respectively, if acting for any other proctor, solicitor, or attorney, shall be subject to the Rules in respect to taking affidavits which are applicable to those in whose stead they are acting.

55. The Registry of the Court for Divorce and Matrimonial Causes, and the clerks employed therein, shall be subject to and under the control of the Registrars of the Principal Registry of the Court of Probate, in the same way and to the same extent as the Principal Registry of the Court of Probate and the clerks therein is and are.

166 RULES AND ORDERS FOR HER MAJESTY'S COURT

56. The Record Keepers, the Clerk of Papers, the Sealer, the Ushers, and other officers belonging to the Court of Probate, shall discharge the same duties in the Court for Divorce and Matrimonial Causes, and in the Registry thereof, as they discharge in the Court of Paobate and the Principal Registry thereof.

57. The Judge Ordinary shall in every case in which a time is fixed by these Rules for the performance of any act have power to extend the same to such time and with such qualifications and restrictions and on such terms as to him may seem fit.

FORMS,

Which are to be followed as nearly as the circumstances of each case will allow.

No. 1.—*Citation.*

In Her Majesty's Court for Divorce and Matrimonial Causes.

VICTORIA, by the Grace of God of the United Kingdom of Great Britain and Ireland Queen, Defender of the Faith.

To *A.B.*, of   in the County of   .

WHEREAS *C.B.*, of   , claiming to have been lawfully married to you, the said *A.B.*, has filed her petition against you in Our said Court praying for   , wherein she alleges that you have committed adultery [*or* have been guilty of cruelty towards her the said *C.B.*, *or as the case may be*]: Now THIS IS TO COMMAND YOU, that within eight days of the service of this on you. inclusive of the day of such service, you do appear in Our said Court then and there to make answer to the said petition, a copy whereof, sealed with the seal of Our said Court, is herewith served upon you. AND TAKE NOTICE, that in default of your so doing, the Judge Ordinary of Our said Court [*or* the Judges of Our said Court] will proceed to hear the said charge [*or* charges] proved in due course of law, and to pronounce sentence therein, your absence notwithstanding.

                            (Signed)   *E.F.*, Registrar.

(L.S.)   .

Indorsement to be made after service.

This citation was duly served by *G.H.* on the within-named *A.B.*, of   at   on the   day of   18 .

                        (Signed)   *G.H.*

No. 2.—*Præcipe for Citation.*

In Her Majesty's Court for Divorce and Matrimonial Causes.

Citation for *A.B.*, of   , against *C.B.*, of   for a judicial separation by reason of adultery [*or as the case may be*].

             (Signed)   *P.A.*, proctor, solicitor, or attorney for the said *C.B.* [*or C.B.* in person.]

No. 3.—*Petition for Divorce.*

To the Judge Ordinary of Her Majesty's Court for Divorce and Matrimonial Causes.

The   day of   18 .

The petition of *A.B.*, of   , showeth,—

1. That your Petitioner was on the   day of   , 18 .
lawfully married to *C.B.*, then *C.Z.*, widow, at   :

2. That after his said marriage your Petitioner lived and cohabited with
his said wife at   and at   , and that your Petitioner
and his said wife have had issue of their said marriage three children;
to wit, one son and two daughters:

3. That on the   day of   18 , and other days between
that day and   , the said *C.B.*, at   in the county
of   , committed adultery with *R.S.*:

4. That in and during the months of January, February, and March 18
the said *O.B.* frequently visited the said *R.S.* at   , and on
divers such occasions committed adultery with the said *R.S.*

Your Petitioner therefore humbly prays,—
That your Lordship will be pleased to decree:

[*Here set out the relief sought.*]

And that your Petitioner may have such further and other relief in the
premises as to your Lordship may seem meet.

And your Petitioner will ever pray, &c.

No. 4.—*Form of Answer.*

In Her Majesty's Court for Divorce and Matrimonial Causes.

The   day of   18 .

A.B. v. *C.B.*

The Respondent *C.B.*, by *P.A.*, her proctor, solicitor, *or* attorney [*or* in
person], saith,—

1. That she denies that she committed adultery with *R.S.*, as set forth in
the said petition:

2. Respondent further saith, that on the   day of
18 , and on other days between that day and   , the said
A.B., at   in the county of   , committed adultery
with *X.Y.*

[*In like manner Respondent is to state connivance, condonation, or
other matters relied on as a ground for dismissing the petition.*]

Wherefore this Respondent humbly prays,—
That your Lordship will be pleased to reject the prayer of the said
petition, and decree, &c.

And this Respondent will ever pray, &c.

No. 5.—*Entry of an Appearance.*

In Her Majesty's Court for Divorce and Matrimonial Causes.

A.B., Petitioner, ⎫ The Respondent, *C.B.* appears in person [*or E.F.*,
    v.   ⎬ proctor, solicitor, or attorney for *C.B.*, appears for
C.B., Respondent. ⎭ the Respondent].

[*Here insert the address required by Rule No.* 13.]

Entered this   day of   18 .

No. 6.—*Form of Subpœna ad testificandum.*

VICTORIA, by the grace of God of the United Kingdom of Great Britain and Ireland Queen, Defender of the Faith, to [*names of all witnesses included in the subpœna*], Greeting. We command you and every of you to be and appear in your proper persons before [*insert the name of the Judge*], Judge Ordinary of Our Court for Divorce and Matrimonial Causes, at   , on   the   day of   18 , by   of the clock in the forenoon of the same day, and so from day to day until the cause or proceeding is tried, to testify the truth, according to your knowledge in a certain cause now in Our Court before Our said Judge depending [*or now before Our said Court depending*], between *A.B.*, Petitioner, and *C.B.*, Respondent [*or in a certain cause or proceeding now in Our Court before our said Judge depending (or now before Our said Court depending), in default of the appearance of*   ], on the part of the [Petitioner *or* Respondent, *or as the case may be*], and at the aforesaid day between the parties aforesaid to be tried [*or in default as aforesaid, between the parties aforesaid to be tried*]. And this you nor any of you shall in nowise omit, under the penalty of every of you of 100*l*. Witness [*insert the name of the Judge*], at the Court for Divorce and Matrimonial Causes, the day of   18 , in the   year of Our reign.

                      (Signed)   *E.F.*, Registrar.

No. 7.—*Præcipe for Subpœna ad testificandum.*

In Her Majesty's Court for Divorce and Matrimonial Causes.

Subpœna of [*insert witnesses' names*], to testify between *A.B.*, Petitioner, and *C.B.*, Respondent, on the part of the Petitioner [*or* Respondent].

    (Signed)   { $\frac{A.B.}{C.D.}$ } *or* { *P.A.*, Petitioner's [*or* Respondent's] proctor, solicitor, *or* attorney.

No. 8.—*Subpœna duces tecum.*

VICTORIA, by the grace of God of the United Kingdom of Great Britain and Ireland Queen, Defender of the Faith, to [*names of all parties included in the subpœna*], Greeting. We command you and every of you to be and appear in your proper persons before [*insert the name of the Judge*], Judge Ordinary of Our Court for Divorce and Matrimonial Causes [*or before Our said Court, as the case may be*], at   , on   , the day of   , by   of the clock in the forenoon of the same day, and so from day to day until the cause or proceeding is heard, and also that you bring with you, and produce at the time and place aforesaid [*here describe shortly the deeds, letters, papers, &c. required to be produced*], then and there to testify and show all and singular those things which you or either of you know, or the said deed or instrument doth import, of and concerning a certain cause or proceeding now in Our said Court before Our said Judge Ordinary [*or now before Our said Court, as the case may be*] depending, between *A.B.*, Petitioner, and *C.B.*, Respondent [*or in a certain cause or proceeding now in our said Court before Our said Judge Ordinary (or now before Our said Court) depending, in default of the appearance of   ],* on the part of the Petitioner [*or Respondent*], and on the aforesaid day between the parties aforesaid to be tried. And this you nor any of you shall in nowise omit, under the penalty of every of you of 100*l*. Witness [*insert the name of the Judge*], at Our Court for Divorce and Matrimonial Causes, the   day of   18 , in the   year of Our reign.

(Signed)   *E.F.*, Registrar.

No. 9.—*Præcipe for Subpæna duces tecum.*

In Her Majesty's Court for Divorce and Matrimonial Causes.

Subpæna for   to testify and produce, &c. between *A.B.*, Petitioner and *C.B.*, Respondent, on the part of the Petitioner [*or Respondent*].

(Signed) $\left\{\begin{array}{c} A.B. \\ C.B. \end{array}\right\}$ or $\left\{\begin{array}{c} \text{P.A., Petitioner's [or Respondent's] proctor,} \\ \text{solicitor, or attorney.} \end{array}\right.$

No. 10.—*Notice to admit Documents.*

A.B. v. *C.B.*

In Her Majesty's Court for Divorce and Matrimonial Causes.

Take notice, that the $\frac{\text{Petitioner}}{\text{Respondent}}$ in this cause proposes to adduce in evidence the several documents hereunder specified, and that the same may be inspected by the $\frac{\text{Respondent}}{\text{Petitioner}}$ at   on   ; between the hours of   and   , and the $\frac{\text{Respondent}}{\text{Petitioner}}$ is hereby required, within forty-eight hours from the last-mentioned hour, to admit that such of the said documents as are specified to be originals were respectively written, signed, or executed as they purport respectively to have been, that such as are specified to be copies are true copies, and that such documents as are stated to have been served, sent, or delivered were so served, sent, or delivered respectively, saving all just exceptions to the admissibility of all such documents as evidence in the cause.

To $\left\{\dfrac{C.B.}{A.B.}\right\}$ *or to E.F., proctor, solicitor, or attorney for* $\Big\{$

(Signed) $\left\{\dfrac{A.B.}{C.B.}\right\}$ *or G.H., proctor, solicitor, or attorney for* $\Big\{$

[*Here describe the documents.*]

No. 11.—*Form of Record.*

In Her Majesty's Court for Divorce and Matrimonial Causes.

The   day of   18 .

A.B. v. C.B.

A.B. did, in his petition presented in this cause, allege that C.B. did, to wit, on the   day of   18 , commit adultery with R.S.

[*Here insert the allegations of the petition.*]

C.B. did, in answer thereto, deny [*insert the denial and any other necessary matters contained in the answer*]. Whereupon the said A.B. denied that [*here insert the substance of the Replication, if any, and so on for the further statements, if any*].

Therefore let a jury come.

No. 12.—*Petition for Alimony.*

To the Judge Ordinary of Her Majesty's Court for Divorce and Matrimonial Causes.

C.B. v. A.B.

The   day of   18 .

The petition of C.B., the lawful wife of A.B., showeth,—

1. That the said A.B. has for many years carried on the business of   at   , and from such business derives the net annual income of £   :
2. That the said A.B. holds   shares of the   Railway Company, amounting in value to £   , and yielding a clear annual dividend to him of £   :
3. That the said A.B. is possessed of stock-in-trade in his said business of   to the value of £   .

[*And so on for any other faculties which the husband may possess.*]

Your Petitioner therefore humbly prays,—

That your Lordship will be pleased to decree her such sum or sums of money by way of alimony pendente lite [*or permanent alimony*] as to your Lordship shall seem meet.

And your Petitioner will ever pray, &c.

No. 13.—*Form of Application under Sect. 21.*

To the Judge Ordinary of the Court for Divorce and Matrimonial Causes.
The application of C.B., of   , the lawful wife of A.B.,
showeth,—

That on the   day of   she was lawfully married to
A.B. at   :

That she lived and cohabited with the said A.B. for   years
at   , and also at   , and hath had   children,
issue of her said marriage, of whom   are now living with the
applicant, and wholly dependent upon her earnings :

That on or about   the said A.B., without any reasonable
cause, deserted this applicant, and hath ever since remained separate
and apart from her :

That since the desertion of her said husband this applicant hath maintained herself by her own industry [*or on her own property, as the case
may be*], and hath thereby and otherwise acquired certain property,
consisting of [*here state generally the nature of the property*].

Wherefore she prays an Order for the protection of her earnings and
property acquired since the said   day of   , from the
said A.B., and from all creditors and persons claiming under him.

No. 14.—*Petition for reversal of Decree.*

To the Judge Ordinary of Her Majesty's Court for Divorce and Matrimonial
Causes.

The   day of   18 .

The petition of A.B., of   , showeth,—

1. That your Petitioner was on the   day of
lawfully married to   :

2. That on the   day of   your Lordship, at the
petition of   , pronounced a decree affecting this Petitioner,
to the effect following ; to wit :

[*Here set out the decree.*]

3. That such decree was obtained in the absence of your Petitioner, who
was then residing at   .

[*State facts tending to show that the Petitioner did not know of the
proceedings; and further, that had he known he might have offered
a sufficient defence.*]

or,

That there was reasonable ground for your Petitioner leaving his said
wife, for that his said wife

[*Here state any legal grounds justifying the Petitioner's separation
from his wife.*]

Your Petitioner therefore humbly prays,—

That your Lordship will be pleased to reverse the said decree.

And your Petitioner will ever pray, &c.

TABLE of Fees to be taken in the Court for Divorce and Matrimonial
Causes.

	£	s.	d.
On every citation	0	5	0
On entering appearance	0	2	6
Filing a petition	0	5	0
Filing an answer	0	5	0
Filing a reply	0	5	0
Filing any further replication to a petition	0	5	0
Filing application for an order for the protection of a wife's earnings and property	0	5	0
Filing application for discharge of such order	0	5	0
Filing interrogatories	0	5	0
Filing answer of each deponent to interrogatories	0	5	0
On every motion by counsel, inclusive of filing the case for motion	0	5	0
Entering order of the Court on motion	0	5	0
Summons to attend in chambers	0	2	6
For entering order of Court on summons	0	2	6
Filing notice	0	1	0
On depositing the record	1	0	0
For the settling of the record by one of the registrars	1	0	0
Setting a cause down for hearing or trial	0	5	0
Entering sentence or final decree in a cause	0	10	0
Entering special verdict, if five folios of seventy-two words or under	0	2	6
If exceeding five folios, per folio of seventy-two words	0	0	6
Entering decree or order in pursuance of a written judgment from the Judge of an Ecclesiastical Court	0	10	0
Entering any decree or order for alimony	0	5	0
Entering order directing how damages shall be applied	0	5	0
Entering order providing for custody, maintenance, or education of children, if two folios of seventy-two words or under	0	5	0
Entering order for settlement of the wife's property, if two folios of seventy-two words or under	0	5	0
If either of the above orders exceed five folios, for each additional folio	0	2	0
Entering any minute, order, or decree in the Court Book other than the decrees or orders before specified	0	2	6
On withdrawal of a cause after same is set down for hearing, to be paid by the party at whose instance it is withdrawn	0	5	0
On the hearing or trial of a cause:			
From the plaintiff	1	0	0
From the defendant or defendants	0	15	0
If the hearing or trial continues more than one day, for each day:			
From the plaintiff	0	10	0
From the defendant or defendants	0	10	0
Producing the Judge's notes	0	5	0

	£	s.	d.
Bill of exceptions signed by the Judge - - -	0	5	0
Entering on the record the finding of the Jury or decision of the Judge - - - - - - -	0	5	0
On every subpœna - - - - - -	0	2	6
On a certificate under the hand of the Judge - -	0	2	6
On every commission issuing under seal of the Court -	1	0	0
Writ of attachment - - - - - -	0	7	6
Writ of sequestration - - - - - -	1	0	0
On lodging instrument of appeal - - - -	0	10	0
Search in Court Books, if within the last two years ' - -	0	1	0
If at an earlier period than within two years - -	0	2	6
In case the Court Books to be searched or the documents required are not in the Registry, in addition to the above -	0	2	6
Filing and entry of remission of appeal - - -	0	10	0
Filing exhibits, not exceeding ten, for each exhibit - -	0	1	0
Exceeding ten, but not exceeding twenty - -	0	10	0
Exceeding twenty, but not exceeding fifty - -	0	15	0
If exceeding fifty - - - - - -	1	0	0
Office copies of minutes, orders, or decrees, Judge's notes or other documents filed in a cause:			
If five folios of seventy-two words or under - -	0	2	6
If exceeding five folios of seventy-two words, per folio -	0	0	6
In case the same are under seal of the Court, in addition for the seal - - - - -	0	5	0
Filing every affidavit or other document brought into Court or deposited in the Registry for filing which no fee is before specified - - - - - -	0	2	6
Taxing every bill of costs:			
If three folios of seventy-two words or under -	0	2	6
If exceeding three folios of seventy-two words -			
When taxed as between party and party, per folio -	0	0	6
When taxed as between practitioner and client, per folio - - - - - -	0	1	0
For administering oaths to each deponent - - -	0	1	0
Examiner appointed to take evidence under a commission for examination of witnesses, for each day's attendance, besides travelling expenses - - - - -	3	3	0

INDEX.

N

O

CPSIA information can be obtained
at www.ICGtesting.com
Printed in the USA
BVHW04*1529280918
528775BV00008B/182/P